THE INVERTED MIRROR

Mythologizing the Enemy in France and Germany, 1898–1914

Michael E. Nolan

Berghahn Books
NEW YORK • OXFORD

Published in 2005 by
Berghahn Books

www.berghahnbooks.com

© 2005 Michael E. Nolan

Library of Congress Cataloging-in-Publication Data

Nolan, Michael E.
  The inverted mirror : mythologizing the enemy in France and
Germany, 1898–1914 / Michael E. Nolan.
     p. cm.
  Includes bibliographical references.
  ISBN 1-57181-669-0
     1. France—Foreign relations—Germany—20th century. 2. Germany
—Foreign relations—France—20th century. 3. Germany—Foreign pub-
lic opinion, French—History—20th century. 4. France—Foreign public
opinion, German—History—20th century. 5. National characteristics,
French. 6. National characteristics, German. 7. France—History—Third
Republic, 1870–1940. 8. Germany—History—1871–1918. 9. World War,
1914–1918—Causes. I. Title.

DC341N65 2004
303.48'243044'09041—dc22

                                                              2004048432

British Library Cataloguing in Publication Data

A catalogue record for this book is available from
the British Library.

Printed in Canada on acid-free paper

THE INVERTED MIRROR

Studies in Contemporary European History

General Editor: **Konrad Jarausch**, Lurcy Professor of European Civilization, University of North Carolina, Chapel Hill, and a Director of the Zentrum für Zeithistorische Studien, Potsdam, Germany

For Elizabeth, who made the endeavor possible

CONTENTS

ILLUSTRATIONS

ACKNOWLEDGMENTS

Every true book is, at some level, the product of a lifetime, but I must limit myself to those directly involved in the genesis and fruition of this one. First of all, I wish to express my gratitude to my Doktorvater Rudolph Binion, whose recommendations, editing, and conversations helped to shape my research and writing. Likewise, I wish to thank Paul Jankowski and Dietrich Orlow for reading and making invaluable comments on the manuscript. Edward Engelberg made much-appreciated improvements to the presentation of my argument. The research for this book would not have been possible without the substantial assistance of the Brandeis University Library. I also wish to thank the helpful staffs of the Widener Library at Harvard University, the Mugar Library of Boston University, the O'Neill Library at Boston College, the Tisch Library of Tufts University, the Boston Athenaeum, the Boston Public Library, the Butler Library of Columbia University, the New York Public Library, and the Bibliothèque Nationale in Paris.

Last but not least, I wish to thank Anya and Sarah for putting up with the occasional fit of crankiness during the production of the book.

THE INVERTED MIRROR

INTRODUCTION

Our virtues are most often merely our vices in disguise.

La Rochefoucauld, *Maximes*

We do not place especial value on the possession of a virtue
until we notice its total absence in our opponent.

Nietzsche, *Human, All Too Human*

Throughout history the enemy has been a ubiquitous figure, though his
manifestations have changed from time to time. It is usually easy to identify him, even in peacetime. He lies beyond civilization, perhaps outside
of humankind itself. He usually lacks the qualities we embrace. His most
ordinary acts are fraught with sinister intentions. Thus, he is a focus of
fear and loathing, and we project onto him our unacceptable feelings and
anxieties. The evil of which he is capable is always far worse than any we
might commit. As adults we remember him as the nameless terror of childhood, the stalking figure who desires our ruin, the specter of our nightmares. Though there may be calculated reasons for our enmity toward
him, it is best not to give these prominence, since rational explanations
lack the necessary passions for opposing the enemy. His annihilation, or
reduction to impotence by whatever means necessary, is the only solution
to the threats posed by him. After all, he would do as much to us should
the opportunity arise. But, paradoxically, though we fear the enemy, we
embrace him as well, because he is a clear focus for the unspeakable
hatreds that dwell within us. It is a cliché of politics that a society without
foreign enemies is a society at war with itself.

The twentieth century witnessed a noticeable sharpening of antagonisms
and an increase of violence in international relations. Advances in the technology of annihilation are only part of the picture. Before World War I,
many observers of the international scene tended to construe differences

Notes for this section appear on page 7.

between nations as signs of superiority or inferiority, strength or weakness. The currency of Social Darwinism and racial theory, reinforced by the experience of colonialism and the carving up of the non-European world by the European powers, encouraged a general sense of a struggle to the death among nations. So the dehumanization and demonization of the enemy became a more crucial part of modern warfare, both hot and cold. Total war demanded a totally evil adversary to justify the enormous sacrifices required. Conflict was no longer confined to the battlefield, and the very existence of the nation seemed to be at stake. The age of world war has left a legacy of violence, genocide, and civil strife that makes it all the more urgent to examine how the concept of the enemy raised the level of enmity between nations. Stereotypes of national character continue to feed international and interethnic conflict in Europe and around the globe. From the Balkans to Kashmir, from the Caucasus to Central Africa, old enemies have been rediscovered and refashioned to suit the needs of nations undergoing bewildering change. At the close of the twentieth century, national antagonisms such as the one that arose between France and Germany at the beginning of the century became the common global currency.

This volume examines recurrent themes in the public presentation in France and Germany of the image of the enemy from 1898 to 1914. During this decade-and-a-half before World War I, each of these two nations projected certain assumptions about national character onto the other by way of creating its primary enemy. Most notably, the qualities each country ascribed to its chief adversary were exaggerated or negative versions of precisely those qualities that it felt to be lacking or inadequate in itself. Banishing of "undesirable" traits and projecting them onto another people was also an essential step in the consolidation of national identity. The Franco-German relationship in these years constituted just such an inverted mirror—a perfect symbiosis of antipathy, fear, and envy. As such, it established a pattern that has become all too familiar to students of nationalism and xenophobia in the late twentieth century.[1]

The critical literature about the mythologizing of enemies and the ways in which they are perceived is surprisingly slight, both in quality and in quantity. It is as if social scientists consider the idea of enemies as inevitable, a fact of nature beyond question, an unavoidable artifact of human aggression. Nevertheless, antagonistic relationships between states have often resulted in striking similarities in mythologizing and image-making about the adversary. The necessity of presenting a stark contrast between "us" and "them" overrides the evidence of reality and militates against a balanced evaluation of facts. What was true for France and Germany at the last turn of the century is relevant to other national antagonisms up to the present day. Thus, this book contributes to filling a major gap in the literature on national enemies generally, as well as that concerned with the Franco-German antagonism specifically.[2]

Mythologies of the enemy were created and reinforced at many different cultural levels. Often the assumptions concerning the nature of the enemy were not explicit, but were clearly present. The sources I will examine in the following chapters represent a wide cross section of opinion in the public sphere. Although some of the sources represent official or semi-official points of view, it would be simplistic and naive to posit image-making as an official process imposed from above. At the same time, to follow the lead of some diplomatic historians who perceive the coarse prejudices of uninformed "public opinion" as a major factor in the coming of World War I would be equally misguided. Whatever one may think of the masses, clearly the decision to go or not to go to war remained firmly in the hands of political élites. Widely accepted stereotypes of the enemy clearly informed *both* official decision-making *and* the response of the general public. The creation of mythologies of the enemy was partly a conscious process and partly a reflection of unconscious fears and desires. The end result was influenced by generational shifts of taste and opinion, political expediency, the vagaries and fluctuations of the literary market, and familiar age-old ignorance and bigotry. Hostile mythologies combined with increasing international tensions to reinforce the perception that war was inevitable, which contributed to an upping of the ante and a consequent further proliferation of hateful images, a cycle that was exacerbated by the outbreak of armed conflict. Wartime propaganda stripped the enemy of any vestiges of humanity and appeared to confirm the worst suspicions and fears of the prewar era.

The concept of "enemy" is clearly an ancient one. Antagonism between different tribes, nations, and societies unquestionably antedated the beginning of history itself. In the modern period, competition between states has taken on ever deadlier forms due to quantitative and qualitative changes among the nations involved. This has become increasingly evident in the past century, as new ways of defining and destroying the enemy have increased the danger of international tensions. Even while the status of "enemy" may be solidly grounded in reality, the image of the enemy belongs to the realm of mythology. It is a strange pastiche of national caricature, selective history, and twisted facts. Real reasons for discord are surrounded by elaborate constructions of fantasy until the original causes of enmity are pushed into the background or even lost from sight.

The mythology of the enemy, what the economist and social commentator Kenneth Boulding referred to as a symbolic image, represents an intellectual shorthand culled from a large array of possible sources.[3] This symbolic image varies incrementally from one individual to another according to background, education, geographic origin, travel experience, and the like. Most people, lacking the necessary education and consumed by everyday cares, are unable or unwilling to think too much about the world beyond a relatively narrow purview. However, in troubled circumstances, even those who should know better may be carried away in the heat of the moment, as they were in France and Germany in the late summer of 1914. The modern world, while successfully addressing more immediate threats such as disease and famine, is nevertheless prey to a vague sense of dread without a perceivable source. The sphere of international relations offers a vista of easily identifiable enemies, and the conviction of national strength and national worth offers a form of security as well as the satisfaction of the apparently universal will to power, even if merely vicarious. As Alain Finkielkraut has noted, echoing Hegel, the need for enemies is also a reflection of the yearning for significance in the cosmic scheme, as the need for heroism and self-sacrifice overcomes the limits of individual existence and the mundane cares of the everyday. Thus, the individual is absorbed into the larger national entity and shares in the apotheosis of the nation.[4] All too often, the individual exchanges the uncertainties of doubt and reflection for the exhilaration of inclusion in the national entity at its "hour of need."

The concept of national character is central to the myth of the "enemy." While they may have a core of truth, broad statements about the "character" of nationals numbering in the millions are tenuous. However, as the sociologist William I. Thomas has pointed out, situations perceived as real are real in the consequences of that perception.[5] There may be superficial reasons for the selection of specific qualities to be emphasized, but the character traits assigned will tend to reflect the real reasons for discord. The growth of national consciousness is often based on a distorted sense of the past, as primary education becomes a tool of national aims, and history is reduced to a tabulation of wrongs and a call for redress. Past and present writers may then be enrolled under the banner of their nation, sometimes without their consent and even with violence to their own convictions.[6]

At the last turn of the century, it was common for French and German writers to refer to each other as the "hereditary enemy," as if national enmity had existed between the two peoples for many generations. Such rhetoric was misleading. Episodes of armed conflict through the centuries did not generate lasting enmity. The German notion that victory in 1870 was just recompense for Louis XIV's invasion of the Palatinate in 1688, or for Napoleon's defeat of the Prussians at Jena in 1806, was more typically part of the German national mythology as it developed *after* unification. France certainly did not consider Germany a "privileged adversary" before 1870.[7] German artists, writers, and scholars had long made the pilgrimage to Paris as the recognized capital of the arts and sciences, and by the middle of the nineteenth century there was a substantial colony of German artisans and tradespeople in the city as well. Fewer French traveled to Germany, but scholars such as Edgar Quinet and Ernest Renan published glowing accounts of German culture. Nevertheless, unfamiliarity with German potential contributed to the French débâcle in 1870.

Educated French readers of the mid nineteenth century learned much of what they knew about Germany from Germaine de Staël's *De l'Allemagne*, published in 1810. Its sentimental portrait of the Germans as a dreamy, poetic, and philosophical people, incapable of decisive action in the world, was overdrawn even at the time it was written. De Staël wished to set her vision of idyllic Germany against the excesses of Napoleonic France, and in the process gave a misleading picture of France's neighbor across the Rhine. Nevertheless, the experience of the Napoleonic wars seemed to confirm her observations. Although Prussia and other German states were victorious in 1813–1814, only as part of an unprecedented coalition were they able to wipe out the humiliations of Jena and Auerstädt. Under such circumstances, the French could afford to be forgiving of erstwhile enemies. The Prussians might be masters of the parade ground, but alone they were apparently no match for French military genius and élan. Heinrich Heine's *Religion and Philosophy in Germany*, written in Paris for a French audience, found an appreciative public. However, few heeded its prophecies of the trouble to come if the Germans were ever able to achieve unity. The same period saw the birth of the notion of "the two Germanys," an idea that had a strong hold in France and even survived into later years. According to this notion, the Germany of poets, philosophers, and composers, the "good" Germany, vied for influence with the "bad" Germany of militaristic Prussia.[8]

The Franco-Prussian War of 1870–1871 radically altered the traditional French view that the Germans were harmless dreamers and second-rate soldiers. In September 1871, following the war, the historian Ernest Renan resumed a correspondence with the fellow biographer of Jesus, David Friedrich Strauss, better remembered for being a target of Nietzsche's scathing criticism of his nationalist opinions and purple prose. The siege of Paris had interrupted an exchange of letters in which the two scholars discussed the significance of the conflict. Strauss rejoiced that victory had demonstrated united Germany's newfound power on the global scene. Renan, on the other hand, long an admirer of German culture and scholarship, was deeply disturbed to see the beginnings of a new trend in international relations: "The stark division of humankind into races, besides being based on a scientific error, few lands possessing a really pure race, can only lead to wars of extermination, "zoological" wars if you will, similar to those waged by various species of rodents or carnivores for their survival."[9] Renan's vision proved all too accurate. The war of 1870 marked the start of a new era of tension in Franco-German relations that was accompanied by ever more ruthless struggles in the international system. This context of mounting belligerency in turn left its mark on the mythologizing process in the Franco-German antagonism.

The defeat of France by Germany in the Franco-Prussian War brought about a radical transformation of the European balance of power. The French, surprised and demoralized by their quick defeat, were forced to re-evaluate their neighbors beyond the Rhine. More than that, as the historian Jacques Binoche has noted, the war brought about "the ruin of an entire intellectual universe which placed [France] at the center of Europe and the world."[10] The Germans, equally surprised by the completeness of their victory, began to make ill-based assumptions about "Gallic" temperament, mistaking their military predominance for cultural superiority, as Nietzsche scornfully noted.[11]

Each country tended to see what it most feared about modernity in the other: France saw regimentation and anti-individualism in the German model, while Germany saw decadence and the threat of disorder in France. By the late nineteenth century, French writers viewed economically and militarily "successful" Germany as inhumanly efficient and militaristic. Concerned by Germany's rapidly growing population and industrial power, French observers equated these developments with their less desirable consequences, such as nightmare urban agglomerations, higher infant mortality, and a proletarianization of the workforce. At the same time, the war of 1870 had clearly demonstrated that France was no longer the dominant military power on the continent. As a result, France became in the imaginations of many French observers the victim of a Machiavellian power play masterminded by Bismarck, the fact that it had declared war on Prussia being conveniently forgotten. By contrast, German writers viewed culturally pre-eminent France as decadent and pleasure-loving, "cosmopolitan" in a pejorative sense of the term, and handicapped by a revolutionary heritage that contributed to instability in politics and the threat of disorder in society at large. Industrial development and population growth lagged behind Germany's, and the economy remained much more rural than that of Germany. Nevertheless, France was still a great power, with an extensive and expanding colonial empire, and continued to play a leading role on the international stage. This apparent paradox rankled many German observers, who thought that the Reich was not playing a role commensurate with its size and strength. Its confused and sporadic pursuit of *Weltpolitik* increased tensions with its neighbors without bringing many tangible benefits. The French feared German power, while the Germans envied French prestige.

The role of the hostility between France and Germany in facilitating the advent of the two world wars is too well known to be recounted in detail here. Reasons for discord were there before 1914, although the outbreak of armed struggle was never inevitable. Indeed, although the years 1911–1913 witnessed increasing Franco-German tensions, from the Agadir crisis in Morocco through the Balkan Wars, the spring and early summer of 1914 seemed to offer less of a threat to peace. The memories of the "beautiful summer" of 1914, subsequently magnified by rueful hindsight, had some basis in reality. Nevertheless, when war did come, few doubted that the enemy was to blame.

At a time when national conflicts seem to be mushrooming all over the globe, the classic case of antagonism between France and Germany offers many insights into similar conflicts of the present. That this *Erbfeindschaft* or hereditary hostility, as it was once widely known, has been overcome gives grounds for optimism that it is possible to adjudicate similar conflicts. History does not repeat itself exactly, but an examination of past tragedies offers clues to avoiding future ones.

Notes

1. The German historian Thomas Raithel has used the term "reverse mirroring" in writing about the projection of aggressive intent by each side onto the other just before World War I. I have taken the mirror metaphor further. See Thomas Raithel, *Das "Wunder" der inneren Einheit: Studien zur deutschen und französischen Öffentlichkeit bei Beginn des Ersten Weltkrieges* (Bonn: Bouvier Verlag, 1996), pp. 105–106.
2. The most thorough recent investigation of the topic of images of the enemy thus far published is Anne Katrin Flohr, *Feindbilder in der internationalen Politik: Ihre Entstehung und ihre Funktion* (Bonn: Lit Verlag, 1991).
3. Kenneth E. Boulding, *The Image* (Ann Arbor: University of Michigan Press, 1956), pp. 109–111.
4. Alain Finkielkraut, *La défaite de la pensée* (Paris: Gallimard, 1987), p. 56.
5. W. I. Thomas *On Social Organization and Social Personality: Selected Papers*, Morris Janowitz, ed. (Chicago: University of Chicago Press, 1966), pp. 154–167.
6. Finkielkraut, *La défaite*, p. 59.
7. Henri Burgelin, "Le mythe de l'ennemi héréditaire dans les relations franco-allemandes," *Documents: Revue des Questions Allemandes* (1979): 77. The myth of the hereditary enemy in both countries was largely a creation of the years 1871–1914.
8. See Beate Gödde-Baumanns, "L'idée des deux Allemagnes dans l'historiographie française des années 1871–1914," *Francia* 12 (1984): 609–619.
9. Ernest Renan, "Nouvelle lettre à M. Strauss," *Œuvres complètes* (Paris: Calmann-Lévy, 1947), vol. 1, p. 456.
10. Jacques Binoche, *Histoire des relations franco-allemandes de 1789 à nos jours* (Paris: A. Colin, 1996), p. 39.
11. Friedrich Nietzsche, "David Strauss, the Confessor and the Writer," *Untimely Meditations*, R. J. Hollingdale, trans. and ed. (Cambridge: Cambridge University Press, 1983).

Chapter One

FRANCO-GERMAN RELATIONS, 1898–1914: A SKETCH

> That which pushes Germany toward war is its inordinate desire for domination, its unimaginable pride and that perpetual distrust, that kind of persecution delirium by which it is possessed. One cannot live in peace with a neighbor who wishes to make you his subordinate and, on top of it all, endlessly suspects you of weaving the blackest of plots against him.
>
> André Mévil, *La paix est malade*[1]

> Resentment against Germany might well be called the soul of French policy.
>
> Bernhard von Bülow, *Imperial Germany*[2]

The diplomatic history of France and Germany between 1871 and 1914 was not one of unrelieved hostility. Relations between France and Germany were relatively quiescent in the 1890s. The Boulanger Affair of the late 1880s, in which a revanchist general seemed to be rallying the French for war against Germany, had seen a renewed increase of tension between the two countries. However, for almost a decade thereafter, relations between the French and German governments became more cordial, if not quite friendly. The chill and hostility of the 1870s and 1880s began to fade, and the prospect of a new war began to look less likely. The Franco-Russian understanding of 1892, which gradually developed into a full-fledged alliance, did cause some unease in Germany, but many German observers believed the relationship between republican France and tsarist Russia to be a quixotic venture that would not stand the test of time, and the Russian army was not yet considered a serious threat to Germany. However, the mythologies of enmity had already taken deep root, and it was difficult to extirpate them from the collective unconscious in a span of only a few years. The interlude was not destined to last.

Notes for this chapter begin on page 20.

Germany's foreign policy in the years before World War I was hampered by indecisiveness, inconsistency, and incompetence. The appointments of Bernhard von Bülow as State Secretary for Foreign Affairs and Alfred von Tirpitz as Navy Secretary in 1897 are usually taken to mark the beginning of German *Weltpolitik*.[3] However, there was little attempt to establish specific goals for this "world policy," nor was there any effort to establish concerted efforts by the relevant branches of the German government and military. No one either within or outside of Germany could say with certainty whether *Weltpolitik* and "a place in the sun," in the famous words of Wilhelm II, implied merely recognition of a German role in world affairs and a voice in crucial diplomatic decisions, or a demand for territorial expansion at the expense of other powers. This uncertainty was at the core of relations among the European great powers for at least a decade before the outbreak of European war and contributed mightily to its coming. The title of a book by Kurt Riezler, a personal advisor to chancellors Bülow and Bethmann Hollweg and one of the more astute contemporary observers of German foreign policy, perfectly encapsulated the dilemma Germany had created for itself by the end of this period: *Die Erforderlichkeit des Unmöglichen* (The Necessity of the Impossible).[4]

The style of German foreign relations during these years did little to calm the fears of other European governments. German diplomacy tended to be arrogant, tactless, and too reliant on the threat of force. A French authority on German politics, William Martin, writing in the wake of the second Moroccan crisis of 1911, saw the typical qualities of German foreign policy as secrecy, indecision, brusqueness, and hostility, hardly a promising formula for diplomatic success.[5] Victor Cambon was one of many who observed that the Germans could not be successful diplomats or colonizers because they were unable to win people over to their cause.[6] German bellicosity on the diplomatic stage found widespread support at home, where much of the press increasingly urged a firm stand on the international scene. The voices of those recommending a pacific growth of German power through economic expansion were relatively few. The Pan-Germanist Heinrich Claß railed against the danger of Germany becoming a larger version of prosperous, peace-loving Belgium, a vision he referred to as "the ideal of those without ideals."[7] While few would today accept without qualification the historian Fritz Fischer's contention that the Imperial German government deliberately risked war in order to head off a socialist revolution at home, it is clear that Germany was more willing than the other great powers to resort to force if it believed itself to be at an impasse. Such an impasse appeared to be at hand in the last years before World War I, particularly with France's ally Russia modernizing its army and its railway system. Whatever the ultimate aims of German foreign policy, France increasingly saw itself facing the sharp end of German power.

The period of relative calm in Franco-German relations was temporarily shattered in the late 1890s by the Dreyfus Affair. The plight of the Jewish captain on the French general staff, accused of spying for the Germans, naturally aroused a great deal of interest in Germany. There was a certain amount of compassion for the falsely accused Dreyfus, especially as his innocence became increasingly clear. Nevertheless, few German observers recognized the relevance of many of the issues raised by the Affair for the political life of Germany. Thus, while the uproar caused by the Dreyfus Affair in France seemed to confirm many prejudices widespread in Germany about the French, most Germans ignored the lessons of the Affair for Germany. The French, for their part, believed that the espionage activity brought to light by the Affair portended renewed German aggression against France.

In spite of the enthusiasm of German liberals for the case of Alfred Dreyfus, many Germans who wrote about the Affair believed that the events in France were further proof of the decline of the French nation, the *Gallierdämmerung*, or "twilight of the Gauls," as one anonymous author styled it.[8] The corruption and apparent degeneration of parliamentary politics in France evoked derisive comments. Otto Mittelstädt, an author who had lived in France and admired French culture, was disturbed by the failure of the republic to come to grips with the Affair. The lack of decisive leadership had allowed a relatively minor scandal to escalate into a crisis that threatened to engulf the republic. Mittelstädt was also critical of the unscrupulous French press, as well as the parliamentary politicians, who he thought had been bought out by "capitalist industrialists." He feared that the only way out of the morass might be a coup d'état, with the probability of a war against Germany to distract France from its domestic troubles.[9] Mittelstädt believed that the ultimate cause of all the agitation was "the flood-tide of half-educated democracy and its demagoguery,"[10] and many middle-class Germans would have shared his view. Maximilian Harden, the acerbic editor of *Die Zukunft*, feared that the worst-case scenario would be a victory of the Dreyfusards and the resulting disgrace of the army:

> If the evidence that Zola wanted to bring out were produced, if the interrogation of witnesses demonstrated that wretched scoundrels stand at the head of the French army, who knowingly pervert justice, allow the innocent to be condemned and the guilty to escape punishment, falsify documents and, without batting an eyelash, commit perjury, then the wrath of the people would sweep away not only this rabble, but also the whole governmental system that could make such an outrageous situation possible, and after a short mob dictatorship, run by groups raised from gutter slime and probably worse in its ravages than that of the Communards, the rule of tyranny would fall to a strong, or seemingly strong, adventurer, a Bonaparte or a Boulanger, whose first priority would be to turn the frantic and convulsive anger of the nation outwards as quickly as possible.[11]

At the same time, criticism of the French army and its role in the Affair in the German press must have found a sympathetic echo among antimilitarist critics in Germany.

As the Affair drew to a close, the prominent socialist Wilhelm Lieb-knecht offered a trenchant criticism of the behavior of the German press toward the events in France:

> Charity begins at home, according to the English saying. And not only charity, but also justice and other virtues begin at home. The press of free countries differs from the press of unfree lands in that it uncovers scandals at home, and only concerns itself with those of other countries afterwards, while the press of unfree countries draws a veil over scandals at home, observing those abroad with a magnifying glass and a microscope. The German press in the Dreyfus Affair has shown its submissiveness with outstanding eagerness.[12]

The ferocious anti-Semitism displayed in France during the course of the Affair surprised many German observers. However, it was clearly not an unfamiliar phenomenon. The anti-Semitic political parties had reached their height of influence in Imperial Germany in the early 1890s. Nevertheless, by 1898 their influence was clearly on the wane. As a result, even German Jews could condemn France for its anti-Semitism and feel fortunate to live in more enlightened Germany. As the historian Ernst Otto Czempiel has noted, the German government and people treated the Affair as a strictly foreign matter, and only later became aware that the larger issues of conflict between military and civilian authority, between reform and reaction, had a direct relevance to Germany itself.[13]

Even as the Dreyfus Affair unfolded, events occurred that seemed to offer an opportunity for a Franco-German rapprochement. The standoff between French and British forces at Fashoda on the upper Nile in the summer of 1898 threatened to drive a new wedge between the old colonial rivals. The eventual French withdrawal was considered by much of the French public to be a national disgrace against a background of internal divisions caused by the Affair. Little wonder then that many in France viewed Britain's discomfiture in the Boer War soon afterward with great *Schadenfreude*. Public opinion in France was almost as incensed as that in Germany by news stories of British atrocities in South Africa, particularly with regard to the use of the newly developed concentration camps to isolate Boer troops from civilians. Mutual hostility toward Britain seemed to offer a hitherto unthinkable possibility of agreement between France and Germany between 1899 and 1902. The international contingent that was assembled under the command of a German general to intervene in China during the Boxer Rebellion seemed to indicate that such cooperation was not beyond possibility. However, the chance for a resolution of differences between the two countries was allowed to slip, and such favorable circumstances did not recur. Instead, French foreign policy under Théophile Delcassé took the fateful turn toward a rapprochement with Britain in the form of the Entente Cordiale of 1904.[14]

The World Exposition of 1900 in Paris seemed to mark a caesura in the progression of Franco-German hostility. During the summer of that year, more German tourists came to Paris than at any other time since the war of 1870. The German press devoted extensive coverage to the exposition. While interest tended to focus on the German pavilion, there were also admiring reports of the organization of the exposition and the construction of Paris's new underground transport system, the Metro. The cordial reception they received seems to have surprised many German tourists. The way to a peaceful resolution of Franco-German tensions seemed open. However, the superficial courtesies of the exposition proved to be mere holiday flirtations.

Between late 1900 and early 1904, a gradual shift occurred in Franco-German relations. While there were no major crises between the two countries during these years, a number of developments hinted at future troubles. The government of Prince Bernhard von Bülow was more willing than its predecessors to practice an aggressive policy toward France. The beginnings of a revival of an energetic and vociferous nationalism in France, especially among educated youth, added a strident tone to public debate on policy toward Germany. German industry, fully recovered from the long depression lasting from 1873 to the mid 1890s, was growing much faster than that of France. Britain's establishment of the Entente Cordiale with France, partly in response to the German attempt to build a battle fleet as a challenge to British naval supremacy, was a worrisome development for the German military and diplomatic leaders. France had emerged from the diplomatic isolation that Bismarck had imagined as the major guarantee of German security since 1871.

The outbreak of war between Russia and Japan early in 1904 marked the beginning of a major shift in relations among the European great powers. The fact that much of Russia's military strength was tied up in its Far Eastern campaign made it a less effective ally of France. At the same time, France was preparing to establish its control over Morocco, an object it had had in view for some years, in order to round out its North African empire. France received British approval for this move in return for recognizing Britain's *de facto* annexation of Egypt in 1882. The Entente Cordiale, concluded in April between the two powers, achieved a settlement of all outstanding colonial conflicts. A treaty with Spain in October set the terms of agreement for a future partition of Morocco. Conditions seemed ripe for France to take the lion's share of the Moroccan prey.

However, Delcassé had failed to take full account of the likely German response to French machinations in the Maghrib. German "policy" in the Moroccan question was a confused amalgam of pique at being left out of negotiations involving several European powers, frustrated colonial ambitions, and a desire to test the strength of the entente between France and Britain at a moment when Russia did not much figure into the equation. On 31 March 1905, Kaiser Wilhelm II disembarked at Tangier and made a short speech in which he defended Morocco's independence and equal trade opportunities for all nations with the sharifate. The consequence was an immediate crisis in Franco-German relations. One week after the Kaiser's visit, the emboldened sultan of Morocco called for an international conference to discuss the future status of his territory. On 6 June, Delcassé resigned as foreign minister.[15]

The Moroccan crisis and the conference were covered in great detail in the French and German press. Reactions on both sides were disproportionate to the relatively paltry prize at stake. As the *Frankfurter Zeitung* noted, Morocco's economic importance to Germany was slight, but its symbolic significance—as a test of Germany's strength on the world stage—was enormous.[16] The *Kölnische Zeitung*, noted for its connections to the German Foreign Office, agitated for German colonial gains in Morocco, but this was more a ploy to extract concessions from France.[17] Morocco did not seem to be an especially promising sphere for Germany to stake a claim. However, a number of German observers, then and later, considered a partition of the country between France and Germany to be a possible option, and one went so far as to envision a plan of settlement for millions of German colonists in Morocco.[18] Later in the year, *Le Matin* ran a series of articles on the relative military capability of France and Germany that noted Germany's greater preparedness for war, and surmised that interests in Morocco were not the only reason for Germany's aggressive posture. Clearly the occasion had been chosen carefully, and differences between the two countries would continue whatever the outcome of the international gathering to determine the fate of Morocco.

The Algesiras conference, a gathering of the European great powers called to settle the conflicting claims of France, Germany, and Spain in Morocco, began in January 1906 and continued until April. The conference seemed to grant Germany's demands for Moroccan independence and free trade. Nevertheless, Germany found itself isolated at the international forum, with only Austria-Hungary as an ally. The crisis the kaiser's government had provoked had clearly redounded against Germany. The imperialist imbroglio over Morocco had several long-term consequences. The relative military weakness of France was glaringly revealed to the French public, providing strong support to those who believed the army was badly in need of reform. The German government, for its part, found itself in a diplomatic isolation that only increased during the following years. Finally, the crisis contributed to a noticeable sharpening of tensions between the two powers, marking the beginning of a period when war gradually came to seem more likely.

The following two years were relatively lacking in dramatic rifts between the two countries. However, the declaration of the Anglo-Russian entente in August 1907 increased fears in Germany that the Reich was being encircled by its enemies. Two events in the fall of 1908, one minor and one major, added to the tension between France and Germany. On 25 September, three German deserters from the Foreign Legion sought the aid of a German consular official in Casablanca to make good their escape to a ship in the harbor. French authorities seized the three by force in spite of the presence of the German vice consul, provoking sharp diplomatic protests from the German government, as well as an upsurge of antilegionary activism within Germany.[19] The second crisis, far more serious, was touched off by Austria-Hungary's proclamation of the annexation of Bosnia and Herzegovina on 6 October. The annexation, though initially agreed to by the Russian Foreign Minister Isvolsky, caused consternation in Serbia and Russia, France's ally. The hardening alliance systems now faced each other for the first time. France and Britain initially backed Russia, while Germany backed Austria-Hungary. Russia finally backed down the following March, when Germany demanded that Russia cease supporting the Serbs and recognize the annexation. Russia was ill-prepared for war, and French public opinion would not have supported a war for Russian interests in the Balkans. However, Germany's room for diplomatic maneuver was clearly narrowing. Germany's adversaries were far less likely to bow to German pressure in future standoffs, especially as all of the Entente powers were devoting increasing funds to building up their military forces, beginning with that of humiliated Russia.

A series of disturbances resulting in the loss of several European lives led to armed intervention by France in Morocco in the spring of 1911. The response of the German government was the dispatch of the gunboat *Panther* to the town of Agadir on the Atlantic coast. This second Moroccan crisis took place in an atmosphere of even greater tension than the first. This time there was little pretense on Germany's part that it was defending Moroccan independence. The German government wanted concrete compensation in return for any acquiescence to a *de facto* establishment of French rule in Morocco. The efforts of Premier Joseph Caillaux to bargain with the Germans behind the back of his foreign minister, Justin de Selves, widely suspected at the time of the negotiations, caused a furor in France when they became known shortly after the end of the crisis. Caillaux was a prominent representative of those who sought some kind of understanding with Germany. The latter included the *parti colonial*, an informal lobbying group of business interests, deputies, and propagandists concerned with colonial affairs. The parti colonial tended toward the belief that the colonies outweighed Alsace and Lorraine in their importance to France, but considered it clearly impolitic to broadcast this belief too widely.[20] Caillaux's adversaries, by contrast, had no such qualms. The convention settling the crisis, signed in November 1911, ceded a strip of the French Congo to Germany in return for German recognition of France's predominance in Morocco. This "resolution" satisfied almost no one in either country, and Caillaux was soon forced to resign, to be replaced by the nationalist Lorrainer Raymond Poincaré.[21]

The second Moroccan crisis opened a phase in which many French and Germans came to believe that war between the two countries was inevitable. Both sides, having backed down under pressure on previous occasions, were increasingly reluctant to do so now, and the possibilities for compromise narrowed accordingly. Caillaux's attempt to forge a working relationship based on compromise between the two countries ran against the stream of preconceived French notions about Germany. Most Germans considered their government to be equally at fault for having raised expectations that could not be met. The cultural critic Oscar A. H. Schmitz wrote afterward that Germany's policy in Morocco in 1911 marked a "failure of reality." Germany could have gotten either a part of Morocco or an alliance with France, but it overplayed its hand and got neither.[22] The press in both France and Germany was much sharper in tone in its coverage of this crisis than it had been six years before. The images that each side had constructed of the other over so many years now began to harden into hostile stereotypes. The period from the spring of 1911 to the end of 1913 marks the apogee of tensions between the two countries.

The decline of the Ottoman Empire in Europe provided the backdrop for the next major crisis between France and Germany, perhaps the most serious before the outbreak of war in 1914. In the wake of Italy's successful war against Turkey for control of Libya, the Balkan states—Serbia, Bulgaria, and Greece—recognized a golden opportunity to achieve their ambitions of territorial aggrandizement at the expense of Turkey's remaining possessions in Europe. The First Balkan War of 1912–1913 seemed to be the beginning of the end of the Ottoman Empire, as the victorious allied Balkan states advanced everywhere and the Bulgarians almost reached the walls of Istanbul. Turkey was a German ally, and its army had received the bulk of its weapons from German armaments firms and its training from German officers. The Balkan states, by contrast, were more closely associated with France, and it seemed that France's ally Russia would press its historic claims to the Straits in the increasingly likely event of a dismemberment of the Ottoman Empire. At a single stroke, German and Austro-Hungarian ambitions in the Balkans and Anatolia, symbolized by the construction of the Berlin-to-Baghdad Railway, seemed seriously threatened. The prospects for a general European war accordingly appeared greater than ever.

In the light of these events, the spring of 1913 seemed to mark the nadir of relations between France and Germany. In March of that year, France restored three-year military service, while Germany upped the peacetime strength of its army. On 12 March, the *Kölnische Zeitung* published an inflammatory article, "Der Störenfried" (The Disturber of the Peace), inspired by the German Foreign Office to drum up support for the new army law, that portrayed France as the fomenter of troubles on the European scene. This article circulated widely in the German press and found a very sympathetic response from the German public.[23] Two incidents that would have been of minor importance at any other time aggravated the situation still further during this period of strained relations. At the beginning of April, a German zeppelin that had developed engine trouble drifted over the French frontier and landed in the town of Lunéville, where the crew faced a hostile reception from the townspeople (see chapter 3, this volume). Less than two weeks later, an altercation occurred between a group of German tourists and some local students in Nancy. The encounter apparently began during the performance of a patriotic, anti-German skit in a music hall, and continued in a nearby brasserie. Tempers apparently ran high, and sharp words were exchanged, though there was no actual violence apart from hats being knocked from the tourists' heads. However, the tourists had to beat a hasty retreat to the train station, pursued onto the platform by the jeering students and a crowd of curious onlookers, while the local police just stood watching.[24] The most striking thing about this utterly ordinary incident was the extraordinary amount of attention it received in the French and German press. In this case, the tendency of the press on each side to report what that on the other side was saying reached almost ludicrous proportions. The fact that such trivial events could escalate into international incidents says a great deal about how deeply the negative images each country had constructed of the other had taken root. These encounters are also revealing in that they represent a confrontations between ordinary citizens, rather than soldiers or diplomats.

Following these incendiary incidents, the rest of the year 1913 witnessed a relative cooling of passions on both sides. As the First Balkan War drew to a close, it appeared to many that a general European war had again been avoided. The centenary of the "Battle of the Nations" at Leipzig, at which the united German states had defeated Napoleon, failed to raise passions in either country. In the fall, an incident between German soldiers and civilians in the town of Zabern in Alsace caused some flurry in both the French and German press (see chapter 4, this volume).[25] However, as the new year of 1914 began, few in either country would have believed that war was on the horizon. The Balkans were far from Paris and Berlin, and not many imagined that a war could result from events in such an insignificant corner of Europe.

Kaiser Wilhelm II

The accession of Wilhelm II to the German throne in 1888 raised hopes in some observers during the 1890s that a new era in Franco-German relations might be dawning. The Kaiser aroused a great deal of curiosity among the French public, which was at least as puzzled, amused, and occasionally alarmed at his behavior and statements as Wilhelm's own subjects.[26] There were numerous books devoted to the subject of Wilhelm, but no one could seem to provide a sure picture of his character and motivations. French monarchists sometimes viewed him as the kind of forceful character that was clearly lacking on the French political scene, but other observers in France were less sure of the kaiser's control over the

German government. André Tardieu, for one, considered the kaiser's actions to be rash and ill-considered.[27] The French public was generally confused by the kaiser's utterances, and never quite certain whether they represented a subtly well-defined policy or mental imbalance. The truth of Wilhelm's indecisiveness and uncertainty would probably have calmed few fears had it been known.

The early years of Wilhelm's reign aroused widespread hopes in both France and Germany for a new era of mutual understanding in Franco-German relations. Wilhelm spoke excellent French as well as English and consistently expressed his desire for a rapprochement with France. There were even rumors of clandestine visits to Paris by the emperor and his entourage.[28] As late as 1906, the writer Jules Hoche expressed his belief that Wilhelm's desire for peace would earn him the title "Guillaume le pacifique."[29] Hoche approvingly noted Wilhelm's conviction that France and Germany were compelled to stand together to prevent the Americanization of the world.[30] However, a number of factors intervened to undermine the possibility of Wilhelm effecting a Franco-German rapprochement. German industrial expansion fueled dreams of German *Weltpolitik*, and Wilhelm could not resist playing the role of cheerleader to German ambitions. The emperor was grossly unsuited to carry out a sustained policy of any kind, but militarism suited his theatrical bent best. It is difficult to avoid the conclusion that the kaiser's emotional instability and temperamental outbursts contributed mightily to the ultimate breakdown of relations between France and Germany and the coming of World War I.

Jules Arren, in his book on the kaiser, correctly noted that Wilhelm's major problem was an inability to believe in the honesty of his critics and in the integrity of political opponents due to his patriarchal vision of an orderly society.[31] Many French observers believed that the Kaiser was strongly influenced by Pan-German circles and shared their exaggerated territorial ambitions. The kaiser's landing at Tangier in 1905 marked the beginning of a negative shift in French opinion toward the kaiser. Wilhelm's increasingly erratic course in international affairs, which Henri de Noussanne attributed to his refusal to recognize obstacles to his fantasies, helped bring about a sharp rise in international tensions during the following years (fig. 1).[32]

Whatever the case, few French observers were able to determine with certainty whether what they were seeing was inscrutable Machiavellianism or truly monumental incompetence. On the eve of World War I, one commentator posed the question of whether the kaiser was afraid of, or preparing for, a showdown.[33] André Mévil thought that the kaiser was a consummate actor, knowing how to play all the roles necessary for his policy, such as the professed friend of France in the early years of his reign and the more aggressive antagonist of later years.[34] The result of growing uncertainty about the kaiser was increasing French distrust of and hostility toward him. Stefan Zweig recalled many years later the reaction of an

FIGURE 1: Are we ready? *I'm ready!* (*L'Assiette au Beurre,* July 1908)

audience in a movie theater in Tours in 1913 when the kaiser appeared momentarily in a newsreel:

> The moment that Emperor Wilhelm appeared in the picture, a spontaneous wild whistling and stamping of feet began in the dark hall. Everybody yelled and whistled, men, women, and children, as if they had been personally insulted. The good-natured people of Tours, who knew no more about the world and politics than what they had read in their newspapers, had gone mad for an instant. I was frightened. I was frightened to the depths of my heart. For I sensed how deeply the poison of the propaganda of hate must have advanced through the years, when even here in a small provincial city the simple citizens and soldiers had been so greatly incited against the Kaiser and against Germany that a passing picture on the screen could produce such a demonstration.[35]

The transformation of Wilhelm from European statesman to the personification of Teutonic evil was thus clearly well advanced in France even before the outbreak of war in 1914, by which point the image of Wilhelm as Germany's chief warlord was well established.

Notes

1. Paris: Plon, 1914, p. 23.
2. London: Cassell and Co., 1914, p. 84.
3. Imanuel Geiss, *Der lange Weg in die Katastrophe: Die Vorgeschichte des Ersten Weltkriegs 1815–1914* (Munich: Piper, 1990), p. 210.
4. Munich: G. Muller, 1913. For Riezler's career, see Wayne C. Thompson, *In the Eye of the Storm: Kurt Riezler and the Crises of Modern Germany* (Iowa City: University of Iowa Press, 1980), and for a brilliant analysis of Imperial Germany's foreign policy dilemmas see Andreas Hillgruber, *Germany and the Two World Wars*, trans. William C. Kirby (Cambridge: Harvard University Press, 1981).
5. William Martin, *La crise politique de l'Allemagne contemporaine* (Paris: F. Alcan, 1913), p. 56.
6. Victor Cambon, *Les derniers progrès de l'Allemagne*, 3rd ed. (Paris: P. Roger, 1910), p. 5.
7. Heinrich Claß, *Wenn ich der Kaiser wär': Politische Wahrheiten und Notwendigkeiten* (Leipzig: Dieterich, 1913), p. 139.
8. (Anon.), *Das Staatsverbrechen des Generals Boisdeffre: Ein Beitrag zur Aufklärung der Dreyfusangelegenheit* (Berlin: Hermann Walther, 1899), p. 5.
9. Otto Mittelstädt, *Die Affaire Dreyfus: Eine kriminalpolitische Studie* (Berlin: J. Guttentag, 1899), pp. 65–67.
10. Ibid., p. 79.
11. "Dreyfus in Deutschland," *Die Zukunft* (26 February 1898): 371. This epic sentence is typical of Harden's style.
12. "Nachträgliches zur Affaire: Schlusswort," part 3, *Die Fackel*, no. 21 (October 1899): 8–9.
13. Ernst Otto Czempiel, *Das deutsche Dreyfus-Geheimnis: Eine Studie über den Einfluß des monarchischen Regierungssystems auf die Frankreichpolitik des Wilhelminischen Reiches* (Munich: Scherz Verlag, 1966), p. 83.

14. See Christopher Andrew's classic *Théophile Delcassé and the Making of the Entente Cordiale: A Reappraisal of French Foreign Policy 1898–1905* (New York: St. Martin's Press, 1968). René Pinon, a prominent opponent of Delcassé's foreign policy, criticized it in a study published in 1913. Pinon considered Britain to be the *éminence grise* of European diplomacy. According to Pinon, the British envisioned the nightmarish possibility of a Franco-German rapprochement during the Boer War and therefore conceived an alliance with France preventively. By sealing the Entente Cordiale, Delcassé limited France's freedom of action, precluding any opportunity to play off Britain and Germany against each other. See René Pinon, *France et Allemagne 1870–1913* (Paris: Libraire-Editeurs, 1913), pp. 107–110.

15. For the first Moroccan crisis, see Eugene N. Anderson, *The First Moroccan Crisis 1904–1906* (Hamden, Conn.: Archon Books, 1966; first published 1930), and Heiner Raulff, *Zwischen Machtpolitik und Imperialismus: Die deutsche Frankreichpolitik 1904–1906* (Düsseldorf: Droste Verlag, 1976).

16. 1 April 1905.

17. See Raulff, *Zwischen Machtpolitik und Imperialismus*, p. 81ff.

18. Rudolf Martin, *Stehen wir vor einem Weltkrieg?* (Leipzig: Friedrich Engelmann, 1908), pp. 49–50. A Pan-German pamphlet appeared at this time with the title *Westmarokko Deutsch!* demonstrating both the poor judgement and the preference for hyperbole prevalent among that extreme nationalist group.

19. There was disagreement about how much political strain the incident at Casablanca had caused. André Tardieu, in his book *Le Prince de Bulow: l'homme et le milieu, la politique extérieure, la politique intérieure* (Paris: Calmann-Lévy, 1909), pp. 151–154, thought the incident had caused disproportionate fuss, while Pierre Albin, *La querelle franco-allemande: Le "coup" d'Agadir: origines et développement de la crise de 1911* (Paris: F. Alcan, 1912), pp. 112–114, saw no unusual increase in tensions resulting from the seizure of the legionaries.

20. Peter Grupp, *Deutschland, Frankreich und die Kolonien: Der französische "parti colonial" und Deutschland* (Tübingen: Mohr, 1980), pp. 72–82.

21. For the details of the second Moroccan crisis, see Thomas Meyer, *"Endlich eine Tat, eine befreiende Tat …": Alfred von Kiderlen-Wächters "Panthersprung nach Agadir" unter dem Druck der öffentlichen Meinung* (Husum: Matthiesen Verlag, 1996); Emily Oncken, *Panthersprung nach Agadir: Die deutsche Politik während der zweiten Marokkokrise 1911* (Düsseldorf: Droste Verlag, 1981); and Jean Claude Allain, *Agadir 1911: une crise impérialiste en Europe pour la conquête du Maroc* (Paris: Université de Paris I, 1976).

22. Oscar A. H. Schmitz, *Was uns Frankreich war*, 7th ed. (Munich: Georg Müller, 1914), p. 32.

23. This article is conveniently reproduced in Otfried Nippold, *Der deutsche Chauvinismus* (Berlin: W. Kohlhammer, 1913), pp. 53–56. Nippold was a prominent pacifist, and this book documents the bellicose stance of much of the German press in 1912–1913.

24. For good accounts of the incident, see the *Frankfurter Zeitung* and *Le Temps* of 17 April 1913. The *Frankfurter Zeitung* also published eyewitness accounts by two of the German tourists the following day.

25. See David Schoenbaum, *Zabern 1913: Consensus Politics in Imperial Germany* (London: George Allen and Unwin, 1982).

26. For Wilhelm's role as an ideal representative of Imperial Germany, see Thomas Kohut's "Mirror Image of the Nation: An Investigation of Kaiser Wilhelm II's Leadership of the Germans," in Charles B. Strozier and Daniel Offer, eds., *The Leader: Psychohistorical Essays* (New York: Plenum Press, 1985), pp. 179–229.

27. André Tardieu, *France and the Alliances: The Struggle for the Balance of Power* (New York: The MacMillan Co., 1908), pp. 151–153.

28. See, for example, Henri de Noussanne, *Le véritable Guillaume II* (Paris: Soc. d'éditions et de publications, 1904), pp. 266–270.

29. Jules Hoche, *L'empereur Guillaume II intime* (Paris: Librairie Félix Juven, 1906), pp. 108–109.

30. Ibid., pp. 238–239.
31. I have only been able to locate the German edition of Arren's book. See Jules Arren, *Wilhelm II: Was er sagt, was er denkt* (Leipzig: Historisch-Politischer Verlag, 1911), pp. 22–23.
32. Noussanne, *Le véritable Guillaume II*, p. 71.
33. Georges Aubert, *La folie franco-allemande: étude contemporaine* (Paris: E. Flammarion, 1914), p. 23.
34. André Mévil, *De la paix de Francfort à la Conférence d'Algésiras* (Paris: Plon-Nourrit et cie., 1909), p. 3.
35. Stefan Zweig, *The World of Yesterday* (New York: The Viking Press, 1943), pp. 195–196.

Chapter Two

HEREDITARY ENEMIES?
THE ONCE AND FUTURE WAR

Wounded in his easily-offended personality, nevertheless he needs a certain amount of effort to demonstrate his anger; he hesitates for a long time and asks nothing better, in order to overcome his last scruple, than to see himself pushed to the limit by others, as Quinet observed. In addition, as the last arrival to civilization, the German has maintained something of a primitive hardness, right into our century, while appropriating to himself all the modern resources of science. We must therefore expect an explosion the more terrible in that it was long delayed.

Alfred Fouillée, *Esquisse psychologique des peuples européens*[1]

Never have relations with our western neighbor been so strained as they are today, never have thoughts of *revanche* shown themselves so openly, and never has it been so clear that the French are using the Russian alliance and English friendship solely for the purpose of reconquering Alsace-Lorraine.... In whatever corner of the world the conflagration might begin, we shall certainly have to cross swords with the French. When that will occur no one can know, but it is certain that the French will use any opportunity to march against Germany so long as they can hope with any confidence to be victorious through the superiority of their own arms or with the help of Russia and England.

"Der Störenfried," *Kölnische Zeitung* (12 March 1913)

The last decades of the nineteenth century and the beginning of the twentieth were a period of unusual quiescence in relations between the major European powers. The last major war involving a European great power was that between Russia and the Ottoman Empire in 1877–1878. However, it was not an age of peace. The most extreme acts of violence were committed against non-Europeans, particularly as the race for colonies heated up after 1880. Colonial conflict also served as competition by proxy, with the unpleasant consequences borne by people who everyone agreed were inferior and who were situated conveniently overseas, where their plight might not attract much notice. At the same time, European culture was rife with images of military conflict, while naturalism and its recurrent theme of the all-importance of heredity in the struggle for existence influenced the perception of international affairs.

The period between 1870 and 1914 was framed by two wars between France and Germany. The so-called Franco-Prussian War of 1870–1871, in which all the German states except Austria engaged and defeated France, established an abiding enmity between France and the new German Empire. The war that broke out in 1914 appeared to many contemporaries, both French and German, to be a direct sequel of the first conflict, a result of its legacy of hostility and suspicion. The notion of a "hereditary enemy" achieved a widespread currency in both countries during the years between these wars. The concept appears at first sight to be a hopelessly confused one. Clearly one cannot inherit an enemy as one inherits genetic physical traits such as the color of one's hair or eyes. The idea of a sustained national antagonism extending back for generations and having as its ultimate result the annihilation of one or the other party was an innovation in European cultural and political life in the late nineteenth century. Domestic enemies could be useful and were plentiful, but social antagonisms among co-nationals could have unpleasant and unpredictable consequences. Foreign adversaries, by contrast, could always be relied on to heighten national unity and distract attention from unpleasant realities at home. The distortion of history was accompanied by a false evaluation of each country's military readiness by the other. French and German perceptions of their respective martial qualities, or the lack thereof, were shaped by their own perceived weaknesses and uncertainties, not always recognized, about the nature of future conflict. Unfortunately, this occurred precisely at a time when a number of new developments made war an even riskier venture than it had hitherto been. The cabinet wars of the eighteenth century tended to be limited affairs, fought by relatively small, mostly cosmopolitan, professional armies and settled by aristocratic diplomats. The wars of the French Revolution saw the introduction of the *levée en masse* and the "citizens' armies." The rise of the modern mass military in an age of nationalist fervor made the concept of a "hereditary enemy" possible, even necessary, as the increasingly bloody demands of the battlefield now required the demonization of the enemy beyond any possible recognition as an individual, sentient human being. Just as the individual was consigned to the amorphous mass of the nation, the complex mutations of history were reduced to an apparently eternal, immutable enmity.

The notion of the hereditary enemy informed much of the image-making in France and Germany before World War I. This was a result, in part, of the establishment of evolutionary theory on the European intellectual scene, already well under way by the time Darwin's *Origin of Species* was published in 1859. The memory of 1870 persisted in both countries, and much thinking about a future war took this past struggle as a point of departure. Very few observers, however, chose to address the technological advances in armaments that had occurred during the intervening decades, making warfare vastly more lethal. The process of building a hereditary enemy was a gradual one, going hand in hand with an increasing emphasis on national identity in both France and Germany. However, once the hereditary enemy was established, it was a relatively simple matter to fit his every action into an overarching plan for revanche, world domination, or other evil. It is a well-known axiom of international politics that the cohesiveness of the enemy's plans and the consistency of his actions are always perceived as greater than those of one's own nation, which (as a matter of course) merely seeks to pursue its own purposes peacefully. It is a persistent problem of international relations that few governments are willing to admit the true motives for their actions abroad to their citizens at home, choosing instead to cloak their real designs with the rhetoric of abstract ideals (e.g., the American way, the German spirit, the Revolution). In the public sphere, accordingly, the actions of one's own nation are always above reproach (at least until overwhelming evidence to the contrary becomes available), while those of the adversary usually have the basest motives. In the post-Darwin era many influential people believed that nations and races, like species of animals and plants, had to maintain endless vigilance and adapt to continually changing circumstances in order to struggle and compete successfully, and the language of evolutionary theory was increasingly employed in the study of international politics and war.[2]

While the period before 1914 marked the high point of racialist thought before Hitlerism in Europe, the dangerous long-term consequences of an international system based on theories of a zero-sum game of evolutionary morality became clear only in the following decades. The experience of colonial conquest and rule over non-European peoples accustomed Europeans to thinking in terms of racial hierarchies, and it was only natural that such categorization would begin to take effect in Europe itself. When the nationalist agitator Paul Déroulède, in a speech of 1908, invoked the image of the French subjected to a hypothetical German protectorate as "des Dahoméens ou des Tonkinois de race blanche," he was utilizing a familiar imperial metaphor of subjugation, raising fears of domination by Germany to stoke the anti-German fervor of his audience.[3] Clearly, the worst fate imaginable to Déroulède's listeners would be subjection to the same kind of servitude endured by France's own subject peoples. It was not uncommon at the time to refer to separate French and German "races"— indeed, the influential racial theorist Ludwig Woltmann, who saw the Germanic root as the essential element of everything great in French civilization, could write that only prejudice and ignorance prevented people from seeing that history was determined by race.[4] While racialism was influential throughout Europe, there were reasons for it to have a special resonance in Germany. German notions of racial superiority were born of feelings of cultural inferiority. French cultural superiority was arguable; German racial superiority was not. By arguing that everything great in French culture ultimately stemmed from the Germanic invasions, the German disciples of Gobineau could claim German credit for past French greatness. Woltmann and others imagined that the decline of the Germanic element and the re-assertion of the "inferior" Celtic element were the root causes of French decadence since the Revolution.[5] The historical precedent was the late Roman Empire, with France as the new Rome offering the splendors of an outwardly magnificent but inwardly corrupt civilization, and the modern-day German descendants of Arminius and Alaric possessing the vitality of the barbarian hordes. The traditional dichotomy of civilization and barbarism was turned on its head, and dynamic barbarism was now considered a force superior to decadent civilization in a world where the racial struggle for survival predominated.

While it might be reasonable to suppose that a hereditary trait comes from nature, clearly nurture plays an important role in the construction of the "inherited" antagonist. The majority of the citizens of France and Germany before 1914 had only limited opportunities for contact with each other, as few had sufficient leisure for travel or study. However, this did not necessarily prevent the formation of elaborate belief systems concerning "them"—indeed, it was far simpler to make broad generalizations concerning a people about whom one knew little or nothing than to attempt to shape perceptions of a known quantity to fit a hostile mold. Paradoxically, it was the growth of mass literacy, and the homogenization of information that accompanied it, that contributed to a narrowing of viewpoint and hardening of opinion toward nations perceived as hostile. The new cult of national history placed one's own nation at the center, banishing others to the periphery, and the standardized history texts of the primary schools imposed a world view of firmly fixed national horizons as well as a simplistic schema of international relations. The daily press and popular literature of the period did much to propagate the received truth that armed conflicts between nations were inevitable, even healthy and desirable, tests of national will. Nor were simplistic perspectives limited to the lower classes. Educated élites too now had to face new realities, though the visions they formed of the society across the Rhine were often only slightly less distorted than those of their social and cultural inferiors.

1870 and After

The Franco-Prussian War of 1870–1871 cast a long pall over relations between France and Germany during the following decades, until it was dwarfed by the far greater bloodbath of 1914–1918. The earlier war made manifest the end of French hegemony on the continent after more than two centuries, and announced the arrival of a new German great power in Central Europe. Contemporaries before 1914 in both countries frequently referred to the earlier conflict as "the great war." The defeat was a deeply traumatic experience for France, while the almost equally unexpected victory was the keystone of a cult of German national invincibility that lasted until the rude shock of defeat in 1918. The experience of 1870–1871 and the question of Alsace-Lorraine may fairly be said to have formed the foundation of Franco-German mythologies of national enmity for the next half-century and beyond. While there had been armed conflict between France and certain German states numerous times before 1870, notably during the wars of the French Revolution and Napoleon, the bitterness associated with past wars had tended to fade over time. The experience of the Napoleonic Wars, German nationalist historiography to the contrary, had not caused a gigantic popular upheaval in the German lands against French rule. It was only in later works of history and literature that the Wars of Liberation gained the status of a great national apotheosis, taking their place alongside the endeavors of Frederick Barbarossa and Frederick the Great. Even so, the cult of devotion that found its culmination in the centenary of the Battle of Leipzig in 1913 was tempered by moderation toward the erstwhile foe, and focused on the glorious memories of Stein, Blücher, and Queen Luise of Prussia, rather than hatred of the French conquerors. The same moderating tendency was gradually asserting itself in representations of 1870 by works of scholarship and literature in both countries. Nevertheless, not enough time had elapsed for hostility associated with the earlier war to dissipate entirely by 1914.

The many novels, plays, historical works, photographic exhibitions, and the like having the war as their subject that appeared in France during the 1870s were almost universally hostile toward the victors of the conflict, who were often represented by caricatures of Bismarck and Wilhelm I as bloodthirsty tyrants. "Le prussien" became a term of opprobrium for a generation, "l'uhlan" the very type of the cruel and rapacious barbarian.[6] It took at least a decade for a more dispassionate and balanced view of the war to emerge in France. This can be said to have begun with the publication of *Les Soirées de Médan*, a collaborative effort by a group of authors around Emile Zola, which included stories by Zola himself and J. K. Huysmans, and, most famously, Guy de Maupassant's "Boule de Suif." These authors approached the war without rushing to judgement, and they did not spare the French from their share of the blame. Indeed, Maupassant displayed a sympathetic attitude toward the Germans, while reserving his more vitriolic attacks for his heroine's fellow French refugees, who are condescending, callous, hypocritical, and overbearing.[7] When the prostitute Boule de Suif patriotically rejects the advances of a German officer, her companions initially support her stand. However, when they are detained and prevented from continuing their flight from the war zone, they grow impatient, and eventually compel her to give in to the officer's desires.

Their snide remarks concerning the patriotic prostitute put them in marked contrast to the Germans, who generally behave decently.

Maupassant's gently devastating portrayal was something of a shock to his contemporaries. Nevertheless, serious works of literature and history concerned with the war mostly continued the trend toward greater detachment and lesser partiality between 1880 and 1914. The historian Ernest Denis placed the defeat of 1870 in the context of earlier French defeats that were not considered disgraceful or definitive (and perhaps hinted at hope of future revanche) when he noted "Après Rossbach, Valmy."[8] Zola, in one of the best-known novels about the war, *La débâcle*, produced a dispassionate analysis of the disintegration of the French army even before it encountered the foe. Zola's war is a sort of natural disaster that descends on France, and he is able to examine minutely the effects of the war on his subjects, Maurice Levasseur and his companions. As soldiers in the French army, they experience the fruitless marches and frightening rumors of the opening weeks of the conflict, and the resulting paralysis and indecision that plague the French forces. Zola treats the events with characteristic detachment. The novel is the penultimate volume in his massive Rougon-Macquart cycle, and his chronicle of the decline of a family under the Second Empire culminates in the application of naturalist method to the depiction of an international conflict that brings about the empire's demise. There is little of the nationalistic outrage that earlier writers demonstrated. Zola's Germans might just as well be Africans or Chinese.

Taking a somewhat different approach, the novelists Paul and Victor Margueritte and Félicien Champsaur could write about the struggle and express hope that a reinvigorated but pacific France would arise in the future, and that such a war, with its evil consequences for both France and Germany, could never happen again.[9] Victor Margueritte's solo effort of 1912, *Les frontières du coeur,* represents a culmination of the trend toward greater objectivity. While Margueritte portrays the wrenching effects of the war on a French family, he nevertheless takes great pains to present the German view of the conflict objectively. Marthe Ellangé, a young woman of Amiens, is married to Otto Rudheimer of Marburg. Marthe admires the austere virtues of the burghers of Marburg and recognizes the genius of German music. At the outbreak of war in 1870, Marthe witnesses the death of her German friend Frida at the hands of a French mob, and judges the incident with the loathing and disgust of the German she believes she is becoming. Nevertheless, she comes to realize that there are "frontiers of the heart" between herself and her husband, who serves as a doctor in the German army, and she shares her family's trepidations at France's defeat and the German occupation. When she gives birth to their son Jean-Pierre, Marthe and Otto grow distant, and she considers raising the boy as a Frenchman. Though they reconcile and she returns to Marburg, a new division has come between them. Otto tries to imagine what it would be like if the situation were reversed and Germany were occupied by France, while Marthe's father reflects on the German qualities of endurance and discipline, which the French will have to learn for the future.[10]

The historian Jules Mazé's account of the conflict, one of the best produced in either country during this period, also conspicuously lacks the invective of earlier accounts. The stress throughout is on the common tragedy suffered by the two countries. Mazé clearly demonstrates that the two sides were more evenly matched than is commonly supposed, and notes that the Germans suffered heavy casualties in the face of heroic French resistance.[11] Henri Welschinger's massive scholarly contributions on the life of Bismarck and the causes of the war of 1870 are still useful works, and notably lacking in patriotic rancor.[12] Eugène-Melchior, vicomte de Vogüé, a prominent literary critic who traveled in Germany and published an account of his observations, could go so far as to conclude that victory in war had inspired the German with confidence in other spheres of modern life, unlike the Frenchman mired in his shallow positivist philosophy.[13]

Nevertheless, there were some notable exceptions to the trend toward greater detachment. Several prominent authors continued to write about the war in a malicious vein. The most striking example of this was Léon Bloy's collection of stories, *Sueur de sang*. Bloy's vision of German barbarism already seemed anachronistic when it was published in 1892. For example, in "A la table des vainqueurs," Bloy takes a page from *Titus Andronicus* by presenting the story of a woman who had been raped by German soldiers and whose two sons had been killed during the war. She becomes a cook in a house where several German officers are billeted and achieves her revenge by murdering the son of one of the officers, a Hessian general, and cooking and serving her prey as dinner to the invaders, who enjoy the meal and rudely shout "Mehr! Mehr, gut [sic] französische Küche!" In "Les vingt-quatre oreilles de 'Gueule de Bois,'" a French patrol surprises and massacres twelve Germans caught in the act of raping a woman in a farmhouse. The corporal commanding the detachment subsequently delivers twelve spiked helmets, each with a pair of ears, to his superior officer. In Bloy's stories the carnage inflicted on the Germans is in marked contrast to the actual experience of defeat. The Teutonic barbarians are distinguished by unlimited depravity, and the extreme violence his French heroes use to overcome the enemy offers a moral catharsis for a lost war. As one critic has pointed out, in Bloy's stories the *franc-tireur* or the partisan is an epic hero, who represents a future that shall overcome an uncertain and dysfunctional present, comparable to the wish fulfillment expressed in many popular fictional and cinematic treatments of the U.S. war in Vietnam.[14]

The nationalist Paul Déroulède, head of the *Ligue des patriotes*, who published his memoir of war and captivity in 1907, noted distinctive shadings of character between the soldiers of the various German states in a way that was already old-fashioned by the turn of the century.[15] He demonstrated some sympathy for the Saxons he had encountered, who seemed to go to war against their erstwhile French allies of Napoleonic times reluctantly, but he found the Prussians and Bavarians to be arrogant and brutal. He recounts an episode of his captivity in which a party of Prussians cruelly mocks him before a portrait of Frederick the Great. Déroulède had initially expressed his malice against the Prussians in *Chants du soldat*, a collection of hymns of hate against the enemy, originally published in 1884, which remained popular for many years.[16] Likewise, the playwright G. Espé de Metz wrote a collection of dramatic pieces about the war that presented the Prussian, personified as Lieutenant Preusskopf, as a figure of stereotyped malice who delighted in torturing prisoners and crushing the skulls of young children under his boot.[17] In general, works such as those by Bloy, Déroulède, and Espé de Metz presented the Germans as amorphous, indistinct personalities, lacking individual will, and cruel as a matter of course.[18] The German soldier usually represented the personification of a well-defined type: the ruthless uhlan, the rapacious Bavarian, the arrogant Prussian. The absence of a well-defined individual character contrasted, of course, with the heroic French soldiers and civilians who were forced to submit in the face of the overwhelming human, or subhuman, flood.

It seems to have been extremely difficult, both in 1870 and after, for many French writers to accept the fact of French responsibility for having impulsively started a war they were unprepared to fight. It therefore became necessary to project duplicity, barbarism, and cruelty on the German foe, who was widely believed to have had a master plan for European domination extending back many years before 1870. A peculiar process of historicization took place in the wake of 1870 in which modern traits, real or imagined, were projected backward and past events reinterpreted to fit a new conceptual scheme. French writers could identify the Germans with Romans (and the French as Gauls defending their liberty), Huns (with the French as Romans defending the empire), or the English of the Hundred Years War.[19] Most French observers considered Prussia the primary nemesis among the German states, however, and pursued the dissection of *le prussien* relentlessly. The sociologist Alfred Fouillée thought he discerned an essential rootlessness in the Prussian character, instilled by the experience of eastern colonization, that made the Prussian subject more malleable in the hands of his rulers.[20] Similarly, the economist Georges Blondel, who sought to warn against the threat posed to France by German industrial expansion, considered the German race as having an essentially invasive character, a legacy of its early expansion into Slav territory.[21] The military writer Maurice Legendre viewed the development of the Prussian state as a perverse accident of historical circumstances, not a true "national" history at all. Legendre speculated on the effects of Prussia's geography and climate on the character of its people, noting that the country was cut off from Mediterranean civilization by its cloudy skies, and that it bordered on a sad and ugly sea, the Baltic, that did not evoke faraway splendors, discoveries, and creations.[22] Such images of Prussia as a chronically bellicose and dissatisfied power were intended as an implied contrast to a France that was peaceful and content. The old tradition of admiration for Frederick the Great, a Francophile even while he was a valiant enemy of France, gave way to disdain for the militaristic tradition whose very personification was the honorary *philosophe* of Sans Souci.

The memory of the war of 1870 in Germany was, of course, vastly different, and in some ways less complicated. The war became enshrined in German collective memory as the most glorious episode of the struggle for German unification. A special prestige adhered to the common victory due to the fact that all the states of the new German Empire participated. The memory of triumph was carefully cultivated in the following decades, with the *Sedantag* becoming one of the most festive holidays and a central patriotic ritual of imperial Germany.[23] Memorials commemorating the war abounded, and many hundreds of historical accounts, memoirs, novels, poems, and plays published after 1870 were devoted to the war. Nevertheless, the ardor of the cult of victory cooled over time. Just as in France, there was in Germany a tendency toward greater dispassion in writings about the war after 1890, and most writers were quick to recognize the merits of the French foe. The sheer number of books devoted to the war was smaller than in previous years, and the tone much more neutral.[24] Perhaps the Germans could afford to be more generous, for they had after all been the victors, and there were more recent successes to celebrate, particularly in the economic sphere.

Fictional treatments of the war likewise tended toward a more neutral stance. The novelist Walter Bloem's popular trilogy of novels shortly before World War I about the experience of 1870–1871 presented a sympathetic view of the French defeat. In Bloem's three novels, most of the German characters, both civilian and military, are magnanimous toward their defeated adversaries. While the French are initially flippant in their expectation of victory, their sufferings eventually arouse sympathy.[25] The antimilitarist Karl Bleibtreu wrote an exhaustive series of short novels about every major engagement of the war, portraying it as a struggle of the French Republic against the militarism of the Prussian monarchy. Bleibtreu could even write a sympathetic account of the Paris Commune as a legitimate defense of the people of Paris against the militarist threat from Versailles.[26] Bleibtreu's opinion flew in the face of the dominant German perspective on the Commune, however, which was overwhelmingly negative, seeing in the revolt of the Communards an event that exposed the anarchic tendencies inherent in French culture rather than an isolated revolutionary outbreak. The deep-seated fears of a certain segment of German society were clearly the dominant factor in the terrified perception of a capital city seized by revolutionaries in the wake of a lost war.

In spite of the increasing objectivity about the war in German novels and histories, certain insidious tendencies persisted in the popular view of the conflict. There was a widespread assumption that the war represented a closed book—that the victory and the Treaty of Frankfurt were abiding facts rather than temporary shifts on the international scene. The war was taught in German schools as the last word on German greatness.[27] The generation of 1914 was raised on the stories of its grandfathers' heroism, and it was widely believed that they would repeat the accomplishment in the event of a future war. Most of all, there was an assumption that, in the wake of such a crushing defeat, France no longer counted as a truly great power. That France had acquired a colonial empire following its great set-back was mainly due to German indifference to colonial expansion during the early stages of the partition of the non-European parts of the globe. The success of France in its imperial exploits seemed completely illogical to many patriotic Germans. Too many had forgotten Bismarck's dual policy of avoiding imperial entanglements while allowing France to seek compensation for the loss of Alsace-Lorraine in colonial expansion. After the turn of the century, when the acquisition of overseas territories became a German priority, many Germans assumed that France and Britain would have to relinquish some of their possessions to satisfy German ambitions, which also encompassed territories claimed by Belgium and Portugal. Such ideas were prevalent across the political spectrum, even among a certain section of the SPD (see chapter 5, this volume). It is clear that the image of past victory contributed to an exaggerated sense of German power and French weakness and the opportunities for exercising German force in a world that had undergone enormous changes since 1870.

The War to Come

The images of future conflict and the preparations for it tell us much about the state of mind regarding war, past and present, in France and Germany before 1914, the influence that the mythologies each country had created of the other had on these images, and the reluctance or inability of most parties in both countries to face the realities of modern warfare. The outbreak of war in 1914 marked the abrupt end of an era of peace and prosperity unprecedented in the history of Europe. The years of peace contributed to a romanticization of war even as new technologies and innovations in armaments made the next potential conflict far more deadly. Not for the last time, there was a cultural lag behind technological development. The imagery of war to come in the public sphere, both fictional and nonfictional, increasingly parted company with the realities of modern warfare. While there was a great deal of interest in military issues, with extensive coverage of the army in the press of both countries, there was little grasp among the public of how much had changed in the conduct of war. As is usually the case, both sides tended to re-fight the last war in imagining the next one. Those civilians who accurately predicted the carnage of the coming conflict remained a small minority, and general staff deliberations concerning the effects of new weaponry were kept secret from the public. The German desire to remove the French threat once and for all and to achieve an unfettered *Weltpolitik*, and the French desire to parry a German offensive and to carry the war into Germany, were both formulated on the assumption that the next war would be much like the last one—short, sharp, and ending in a single decisive battle and total victory for one side or the other. The cheering crowds of the late summer of 1914 shared the illusion of a short war and a quick decision, with a minimum of disturbance to the established order.

It is difficult to determine exactly how most French and Germans before 1914 envisioned the coming war. Nevertheless, it seems reasonably certain that most anticipated that if war could not be avoided it would last only a few months, as it seemed impossible that a war could last longer in the modern age without catastrophic consequences for all the countries involved. The well-known authors Norman Angell and Ivan Bloch, whose works were translated into French and German and who argued that a major war between great powers was impossible due to the dislocations it would cause to the world economy, may have contributed unintentionally to lulling public opinion into a false sense of security. Thus, hawks and doves alike contributed to an atmosphere in which a protracted conflict came as an unpleasant surprise.

There was a strong tendency in Germany, based on the experience of 1870, to underestimate French military capability. The Pan-Germanist and Baltic German writer Paul Rohrbach expressed the opinion of many Germans when he downplayed the French threat, considering Britain as the primary enemy. While admitting that French troops had courage and dash, Rohrbach clearly thought that German discipline and application were more than a match for these qualities.[28] The case of an officer of the German General Staff destined to play a tragic role in Franco-German relations offers interesting insights. Colonel Erich von Falkenhayn was an admirer of French culture and spoke fluent French. He spent the early months of 1910 in Paris, where he renewed the acquaintance of Colonel Louis Eugène Arlabosse, whom he had met when stationed in China at the turn of the century. While demonstrating a warm friendship for Arlabosse and others he met in Paris at that time, and appreciating the pleasures of the French capital, Falkenhayn was very negative in his evaluation of modern France and its ability to maintain itself as a great power. He came to the conclusion that France had learned little from its experiences in the previous war, and that the French army was no match for its German counterpart. Falkenhayn's inability to evaluate French military strength accurately was widely shared in German government and military circles even after the outbreak of war, and played a major role in Falkenhayn's decision, as head of the General Staff after September 1914, to engage France in a campaign of attrition at Verdun in 1916. The assumption that

France could be defeated relatively quickly, leaving Britain as the sole adversary in the west, proved to be a gross miscalculation for both sides. The possibility that the French army might be a tough nut to crack seems to have been discounted.[29]

The German conviction that France was a power in decline, with stagnating population growth and tumultuous political struggles that compromised military preparedness, was based on outdated notions that failed to take new realities into account. The Dreyfus Affair had indeed reflected poorly on the French officer corps, and the antimilitary novels that appeared in France during the 1890s were an expression of antimilitarist sentiment not confined to a handful of intellectuals. A German handbook on the French army published shortly after the Affair conjectured on the uncertainty of discipline holding in the French army in the event of war.[30] However, the Moroccan crisis of 1905 spurred efforts to reform the French army, and the reaction of public opinion to the *affaire des fiches* of 1906, in which it was revealed that the government of Emile Combes was attempting to keep tabs on officers not considered reliable republicans, demonstrated a strong undercurrent of support for the army among the French public. The nationalist revival that took place in France after 1905 also contributed to the rising status of the French officer corps. The last uncertain factor, the behavior of French socialists in the event of war, was decided by the Germans themselves when they invaded, providing the extraordinary circumstance that brought about a temporary respite in political and social struggles in France.[31]

The French perception of the German military threat was more complex, but equally beset by delusions. Only a few observers predicted a drawn-out struggle, a war of tooth and claw.[32] The military expert Paul Combes predicted that a German invasion would probably come at a moment when it was least expected, and that the diplomatic crisis preceding it would be exceedingly brief, giving France little time for advance preparation.[33] It is interesting to note that a number of observers correctly predicted a German offensive through Belgium.[34] One author could even predict that the future German offensive would necessitate an initial withdrawal of the French army to prevent its annihilation.[35] Nevertheless, many observers believed that the French army was adequate to face any threat from the German juggernaut because of the superior individual qualities of the French soldier. In his book describing intellectual trends and attitudes among German youth, André François-Poncet described what he considered the innate respect for power and force in the German character, as well as the stunting effects of blind obedience and excessive discipline on the personality and individuality of young Germans.[36] The military writer Arthur Boucher speculated that Germany's very overconfidence might be its greatest weakness.[37] The authors of one fantasy novel envisioned a future struggle in which the French army, reduced to 70,000 by pacifist and Church influence, nevertheless succeeds in trapping and annihilating a German army at Sedan![38] Few experts considered the consequences of failure of either army to prevail, and those that did still could not grasp the full reality of the looming massacre. Maurice Legendre thought that there were worse things than the bloody death of a generation on the battlefield, such as dying young of tuberculosis or alcoholism, or succumbing to the "poverty of blood" brought about by industrialism.[39] The pacifistically inclined economist Georges Aubert, who spent five years of his youth traveling through Germany as a commercial agent, may have been closer to the truth than he realized when he envisioned a future war in which French and German qualities would cancel each other out, leading to a complete deadlock that would leave no option but compromise.[40] In the event, many of these predictions proved to be accurate, but the result was a protracted conflict seemingly without end rather than a quick showdown.

A curious affair of 1903 that attested to what some in France believed to be the excessive militarization and taste for obedience of German society attracted some interest in the French press. A confidence trickster posing as a Prussian officer took command of a detachment of soldiers, marched them to the town hall of Köpenick in the suburbs of Berlin, and demanded an inspection of the town's account books. Claiming to find an irregularity, the "captain" commandeered the funds in the town's treasury. Vowing to initiate an investigation, the officer marched off with the confiscated money, never to be seen again. French observers were even more amused than their German counterparts at this display of obsequiousness toward a uniform. The incident seemed to confirm to French minds that the Germans were unthinking marionettes lacking in individual judgement and excessively deferential toward authority figures.[41]

A certain self-induced myopia imposed itself on both the French and German armies regarding the nature of the next war. While there was a great deal of awareness and debate among general staff officers in both countries concerning the tactical consequences of armaments innovations, there was also a reluctance to recognize the changing realities of modern combat. Public awareness of these debates was very limited. The operational plans of the two countries in the event of a major war, as they emerged before 1914, reflected the preference for the short-war illusion shared by the respective general staffs.[42] The Schlieffen Plan, originally developed by Alfred von Schlieffen, called for a German invasion of France through Belgium that would outflank the French armies and destroy the enemy in a matter of weeks. The French Plan XVII called for an attack through Alsace and Lorraine that would then push deep into German territory. Plan XVII was largely a result of the influence of Colonel de Grandmaison, an instructor at the Ecole de Guerre who stressed the need for an *offensive à outrance*. The Schlieffen Plan and Plan XVII were both flights from the looming reality of a long war of materiel into comforting fantasies of rapid offensives that would decide the war at the outset. One historian has noted that the German General Staff after Schlieffen embraced Schlieffen's plan even in the face of the strongest evidence that it could not succeed, because there seemed no other workable plan to solve Germany's strategic predicament.[43] Mythologies of national character contributed a great deal to the genesis of these plans. Schlieffen's design had as its aim the replay of the German victory of 1870, with the assumption that the French had learned nothing and would oblige with a repeat performance of their earlier débâcle, only this time succumbing even more quickly.[44] Grandmaison argued that the Germans must at all costs be denied the initiative that had been theirs in the previous war. The Grandmaison doctrine of the *offensive à outrance* had as its aim the countering of German *Methodik* with French élan and cold steel, which would overcome more prosaic weapons such as machine guns and heavy artillery. Once the Germans were checked by the French advance, their relative lack of flexibility and individuality would begin to tell against them, and the *furia francese* could be carried into the heart of Germany. Both Plan XVII and the Schlieffen Plan represented extraordinary flights of fancy on the parts of the French and German general staffs, and only the staggering losses of the first months of the war bought an end to these pipe dreams of quick victory.[45]

The vision of war to come took perhaps its most fantastic form in Adolf Sommerfeld's *France's End in the Year 19??* a popular book published in Germany in 1912.[46] In his fanciful, detailed account, Sommerfeld projected aggressive intent onto France: war breaks out when the French torpedo a German gunboat off the coast of Morocco. Britain and Russia, appalled by this French provocation, refuse to stand by France as members of the Triple Entente, this being strictly a defensive alliance. Italy, on the other hand, joins its partners in the Triple Alliance for the invasion of France, which is overwhelmed in short order. In spite of several bloody battles, and the use of various innovations from airplanes to Senegalese troops, the French succumb in a matter of weeks. Germany establishes a brutally repressive regime, annexing much of eastern France, but only in response to blatantly illegal guerilla activity by the French. Thus, the threat from France is forever quelled, and German predominance on the European continent is now unchallenged. Such a vision of a war against France as gloriously brief found an enthusiastic audience among the German public, and one can only surmise that the German General Staff must have found Sommerfeld's book pleasant reading.

The Foreign Legion

One long-established French military institution that received a great deal of bad publicity in Germany was the Foreign Legion. The affair of the German deserters from the Legion in Casablanca in 1908, though relatively muted in both the French and German press at that time, did nothing to improve the Legion's poor reputation across the Vosges, and rumors of kidnapping of young German men for impression into its ranks were rife in 1909.[47] To many German observers, the Legion seemed to be yet another method that France was using to make up for its shortage of manpower, such as the alliance with Russia, the recruitment of an *armée noire* in Africa, or the adoption of three-year service. Worse, it appeared that German youth were being lured by tales of adventure in exotic lands to serve in the pay of Germany's enemy, where they faced death securing France's empire of desert wastes. The fact that some of these young men were avoiding military service in Germany was an additional point of contention. There were several antilegionary organizations in Germany devoted to persuading German youth not to become mercenaries in French pay. French observers, by contrast, resented what they perceived as interference by the German government in what was, after all, a voluntary military formation composed of soldiers of many different nations and having a long and glorious history behind it.

German publications about the Legion in the wake of the affair of the deserters in Casablanca included fictional accounts as well as memoirs of men who had served in its ranks. One of the most popular accounts was *In der Fremdenlegion* by Erwin Rosen.[48] Rosen was a classic candidate for the Legion who had lived in the United States for several years, where he learned to ride and shoot in Texas and became a reporter for a German-language newspaper in St. Louis. He eventually returned to Germany and married, but found the more mundane life there constricting, and his marriage ended in divorce. Depressed, he decided to join the Legion to forget his troubles. Rosen's account is a lively description of life in the Legion, and he does not seem to have suffered unduly from the experience. It was his opinion, however, that most of the recruits were German, and that France was receiving tremendous benefits from them at a small price.[49] Clearly the risks these soldiers ran were not worth the pittance they received in pay. Rosen eventually succeeded in deserting the Legion and returning to Germany.

A popular novel about the Legion was Max Geißler's *Valentin Upp, der Legionär: Nach Berichten eines alten Afrikaners.*[50] Valentin, a young, honest, and slightly dim-witted Prussian, younger son of a farming family, decides to set off on his own in the world. On his travels, he meets Richard von Zahn, a footloose Lorrainer and veteran of the Legion who persuades him to join up. Valentin acquits himself well, surviving a furious battle with the Berbers in the desert and finding his way back to base after becoming separated from his company.[51] Nevertheless, the realization gradually dawns on him that he is serving in a regiment of Germany's hereditary enemy, and he determines to desert at the first opportunity.[52] Valentin succeeds in escaping to the coast and boarding an Italian steamer, but he thinks sadly of his German comrades trapped in the burning desert, where they face death in battle preserving France's colonial empire.

The brutal reputation of the Legion in Germany had some basis in reality, but discipline in the Legion was hardly worse than that in the German army, as some French observers noted.[53] Clearly other factors were at work in the growing German hostility toward the Legion. The Legion seemed to many Germans to be an institution that was against nature, an anachronistic band of mercenaries in the style of Renaissance Italy or of Germany in the Thirty Years War, a multinational *soldatesca* that served to expand and maintain France's large colonial empire while France's own population stagnated. It was widely believed that France used the Legion to enjoy the fruits of its empire on the cheap, sparing its own sons the harshness of desert campaigns. Germans viewed the Legion with unease precisely because it was apparently so successful in an era when national armies were the rule and serving under one's own flag was counted a sacred duty.[54] It was also widely feared that Germans recruited into the Legion might one day find themselves fighting against their own country.[55] Whatever the case, antilegionary sentiment persisted in Germany, as was shown by a large gathering of the *Hilfsverband gegen die Fremdenlegion* in Berlin in April 1914.[56]

Espionage

There was enormous interest in espionage in both France and Germany before World War I, and it was a popular theme of pulp novels, adventure stories, and the like. There was greater concern about German spy activity in France than about French espionage in Germany, partly because there was a widespread impression in France that the Germans were particularly active in this field, and partly because of the apparent disruption of French intelligence in the wake of the Dreyfus Affair. There was, therefore, a great deal of anxiety in France that Germany was establishing a network of military espionage that would be extremely useful in the event of a new war between the two powers.[57] A number of factors contributed to the greater concern about German spies in France. The Dreyfus Affair was the last, and most spectacular, of a series of espionage scandals that shook France in the 1890s.[58] In the aftermath of the Dreyfus Affair, some right-wing writers excoriated France's republican institutions and political corruption for making the country more vulnerable to spies. More important, however, was the perception that the German reputation for efficiency and assiduity in research, well-known in the spheres of commerce, industry, and academia, extended to intelligence gathering as well.[59] Ironically, the Dreyfus Affair demonstrated to those in the know on both sides that, while German embassy officials were indeed carrying on espionage activity, it was a rather amateurish and not very successful effort, often relying on shadowy figures of doubtful reputation and veracity.

Although known facts concerning German agents in France were few, the popular imagination filled the gaps in real knowledge with fearful conjecture. Rumors were rife that the northeastern departments were full of German spies who had been established in France for many years as tradesmen and shopkeepers, working to obtain the good will of their clients.[60] It was believed that these agents gathered as much information as possible concerning invasion routes, railroads, fortifications, mines, and factories. Just as it was widely accepted that some "Alsatians" had turned out to be Prussian spies in 1870, so now it seemed clear that German agents were waiting for the moment of invasion to emerge from deep cover and begin a campaign of sabotage and sowing confusion.[61] It was an article of popular faith in France that the French were incapable of the duplicity required for this activity at which the Germans were so talented, though this seemed to contradict another popular stereotype of the German as ponderous and somewhat slow-witted. Apparently the paradigm shifted as needs required.

One of the more peculiar works devoted to the subject of German espionage in France was Léon Daudet's *L'avant-guerre: études et documents sur l'espionnage juif-allemand en France depuis l'affaire Dreyfus*, which received a great deal of attention following its publication in 1913.[62] The son of the writer Alphonse Daudet, this nationalist and rabidly anti-Semitic author proposed to prove that "German" Jews had infiltrated those branches of French commerce and industry pertaining to national defense.[63] Daudet accused Lucien Baumann, the head of the Société des Grands Moulins de Corbeil, which supplied much of Paris's flour, of being a "German" Jew who was not to be trusted in the event of war. (Baumann was actually Alsatian by origin.) Daudet also claimed that German coal was sold to French fortresses below market price in order to establish a monopoly with the double purpose of weakening French defenses in the event of war and causing unemployment among French miners and resultant civil disorders at the whim of Germany.[64] Noting that a German conglomerate participated in the exploitation of iron mines in Normandy, Daudet asked if France would continue to provide iron ore to "the God Arminius and the factories of Krupp."[65] Not everyone who took Daudet's charges seriously was on the lunatic fringe of the right. The conflation of German and Jew revealed the lingering effects of the Dreyfus Affair on French consciousness, and Daudet's book caused widespread concern among his contemporaries.

Fear of spies, traitors, and saboteurs was nothing new on the European scene. However, the increasing development of national identities and the technological advances of modern warfare made it appear that more was at stake in the game of espionage than ever before. Spy mania reached new heights after the outbreak of war in 1914. Nevertheless, the prewar years had laid the foundations for a realm of fictional and nonfictional spy mania that has become an area of great popular interest in the twentieth century.

War in the Air

In the last years before the outbreak of war, French and Germans were forced to take into account a new factor of military power: aerial warfare. The development of airplanes and airships seized the popular imagination with visions of futuristic flying machines piloted by a new generation of knights errant, but it also caused tremendous anxiety concerning the possibility of death inflicted from the air. The incident of a forced landing by a zeppelin with a damaged motor in the town of Lunéville in the spring of 1913 revealed many of the tensions simmering between the two countries as well as the fear inspired by German airships. While German press coverage of the unexpected arrival of the airship Z-4 in Lunéville stressed the correct behavior of French officials toward the German crew, French papers reported on the hostility of the crowd that gathered, which jeered and threw stones at the car carrying the German officers to the *mairie*.[66] The French were clearly worried about the potential for destruction raining down from the skies, and the sheer size of the zeppelins made them seem a particularly potent menace. One expert on the subject of air power attempted to warn the French public against complacency in the face of the German head start in airship design and operation.[67] However, the Germans were also prone to flights of fancy concerning French air machines. In his imagined rendition of the war to come, Adolf Sommerfeld envisioned a French attempt to break out of a new siege of Paris by way of an aerial fleet hastily constructed in the capital, reminiscent of the balloonists of 1870. However, the Germans foil the French plan by firing shells filled with poison gas at the French aircraft, killing the pilots.[68]

The new frontier of air war represented the cutting edge of military technology, and both French and Germans invested a great deal in its development. The fact that the Germans initially focused on airships, while the French chose to build airplanes, made it more difficult for each side to evaluate the other's capabilities in the air. Nevertheless, in spite of the cachet of aviators among the general public, few senior officers on either side took the potential of these new war machines seriously. Their real possibilities became clear only after the outbreak of war.[69]

Conclusion

The hostility that existed between the two countries sometimes startled contemporaries when it was manifested at the individual level. Victor Klemperer, the scholar of romance languages, recalled in his memoirs an episode from his travels in France shortly before the war. In Saint-Malo he encountered a young French officer, Lieutenant Alfred Chavanne, who gave him a tour of the town. During their time together, they discovered a shared interest in literature and entered into a protracted, seemingly friendly, discussion. However, when Klemperer suggested that France and Germany could get along as well as the two of them, his new friend contradicted him. After spending the rest of the afternoon together without speaking much, the two went to a restaurant to dine.

> Then, immediately after the last bite, Chavanne took on a stiff and almost ceremonious bearing. He said he must now give me an explanation. Two years before a German gentleman had very graciously given him a tour of Berlin. At the time he pledged to himself to pay back this kindness to some German traveler in France. "I have done that this afternoon. Therefore I am now even with Germany." And before I could recover from my amazement, he had placed the money for his share on the table, nodded to the waiter, and with a small bow toward me, left the restaurant without offering me his hand.[70]

In a similar fictional account (though, one would like to think, based on an actual meeting) the poet Ernest Raynaud described in verse an encounter with a potential adversary:

Je te parle. Tu me causes.	I talk with you. You chat with me.
Mais l'histoire a tellement,	But, you see, history has
Vois-tu, compliqué les choses	Complicated matters so
Que notre sourire ment.	That our smiles lie.
Ta bonne obligeance en somme	Your civility, in sum
Ne me flatte qu'à moitié;	Charms me only partially;
J'ai peur d'y démêler comme	I fear I may see in it
Un effet de la pitié.	An effect of pity.
Tant qu'un retour d'équilibre	As long as no return of peace
Ne nous aura pas permis	Permits us
D'échanger une âme libre,	To consent as free spirits,
Nous resterons ennemis.	We shall remain enemies.
Et je me dis que peut-être	And I tell myself that
L'un et l'autre, si demain	If perhaps tomorrow
Nous voit à nouveau paraître,	Sees us meet again,
Ce sera l'arme à la main.[71]	It will be with arms in hand.[71]

Both encounters, factual and fictional, reflect a tendency that was widespread in France and Germany of the period, an inability to see the would-be adversary as an individual rather than as a member of the opposite nation, imbued with an elaborate baggage of history and heredity in the form of preconceived character traits representing a strange inversion of the observer's own perceived qualities. It is this inverted mirroring that is one of the most striking aspects of French and German perspectives of each other before World War I.

In March 1913, as the Balkan Wars raised tensions in Europe to a fever pitch, the *Kölnische Zeitung*, a newspaper noted for its ties to the German Foreign Office, published a major article branding France as "the disturber of the peace."[72] This article resonated through the German press, which took up the theme of Germany's encirclement and the danger of an attack from the Triple Entente if Germany should find itself at a disadvantage. In retrospect, it seems clear that the German government was preparing the way for an offensive at the outbreak of a war it assumed to be inevitable. By 1914, most military experts in Germany believed that a war in the short term offered better prospects of German success than a struggle put off to an indeterminate future, when France and especially Russia would have a relatively greater advantage. The projection of aggressive intent on Germany's western neighbor was an important prerequisite for the contingency of an earlier war. While few still accept the original Fischer thesis of a deliberate German policy to provoke war, dictated primarily by domestic political considerations, it is clear that Germany was more willing to risk war than the other European powers. However, the entire German design hinged on a gross underestimate of France's ability to withstand a German assault. The shattering of German hopes for a quick victory at the Battle of the Marne did not extinguish hopes among the general public that the French would ultimately yield, although privately many senior staff officers believed a total victory of arms impossible. In spite of such doubts, the likelihood of a negotiated settlement receded as the fighting continued and casualties mounted, month by month, then year by year. Both sides found themselves trapped in the contradictions of policies based largely on ill-founded assumptions of the adversary's weaknesses and misguided assumptions about national character.

In short, attitudes toward war, past and present, reflected the more general complex of attitudes of French and Germans toward each other. Though there was much insistence in both countries that the war must not be lost, there was little consideration of the possible consequences of defeat. The French believed that 1870 was a historical accident, and that French élan and individual initiative would overcome the rigid and inflexible German war machine. The Germans judged 1870 as a historical sea change, with Germany inevitably triumphing over a decadent France. They believed they would duplicate the feat on a larger scale in the future, and considered German efficiency and method clearly superior to French indiscipline. Rarely was the inversion of national qualities, real and imagined, on both sides so clear as in the military sphere. Neither side could rid itself of preconceived notions of the other largely derived from 1870–1871, and both failed to realize that the very weaknesses they were projecting might not correspond to reality. This was particularly so given the changed circumstances of modern warfare, which only became fully clear once the war began. These failures of judgement must be seen as a contributing factor in the coming of a war that decimated both countries and poisoned relations still further. The very impossibility of accepting defeat determined the brutality of the conflict in advance, reduced the possibility of an early end to the war by mutual agreement, and virtually ensured future conflicts out of a reluctance on either side to accept defeat.

Notes

1. 5th ed. (Paris: Félix Alcan, 1914), p. 303.
2. For a contemporary example, see Victor César Eugene Dupuis, *L'évolution militaire en Allemagne et en France: Essais de sociologie militaire* (Paris: G. Kleiner, 1901), p. 8; see also D. P. Crook, *Darwinism, War, and History: The Debate over the Biology of War from the 'Origin of Species' to the First World War* (Cambridge: Cambridge University Press, 1994).
3. Cited in Raoul Girardet, ed., *Le nationalisme français, 1871–1914* (Paris: Editions du Seuil, 1983), p. 226.
4. Ludwig Woltmann, *Die Germanen in Frankreich: Eine Untersuchung über den Einfluss der germanischen Rasse auf die Geschichte und Kultur Frankreichs* (Jena: E. Diederichs, 1907), pp. 7–8. Woltmann actually undertook a tour of France to view portraits, death masks, and other portrayals of French nobles and create a catalogue of traits of genius that could be linked to the Germanic origins of the French nobility.
5. Ibid., pp. 109–118.
6. The term *boche* was coined in the 1870s, but it achieved widespread popular currency only after 1914. No similar term for the French was in common use in Germany. *Welsch*, which occasionally has a pejorative connotation, did not become a popular term of abuse. Alsatians were sometimes pejoratively referred to as *Wackes*. See Wolfgang Leiner, *Das Deutschlandbild in der französischen Literatur* (Darmstadt: Wissenschaftliche Buchgesellschaft, 1989), p. 183ff., and the delightful book by Paul Posse, *Die Boches: Eine Culturschande in System gebracht (Eindrucksvoll vertieft durch Meisterwerke der künstlerischen Sektion für Bochologie)* (Gedruckt im Narrenmond; Leipzig: Georg Kummers Verlag, 1928).
7. Emile Zola *et al.*, *Les Soirées de Médan* (Paris: Fasquelle, 1955).
8. Ernest Denis, *La fondation de l'empire allemand, 1852–1871* (Paris: A. Colin, 1906), p. v.
9. Paul and Victor Margueritte, *Le désastre* (Paris: Plon-Nourrit, 1898) and Félicien Champsaur, *L'Abattoir (1870–1871)* (Paris: L'Ermitage, 1910).
10. Victor Margueritte, *Les frontières du coeur* (Paris: Flammarion, 1912).
11. Jules Mazé, *L'année terrible: la défense de Paris: armées du nord, des Vosges et de l'est* (Tours: A. Mame, 1909).
12. Henri Welschinger, *Bismarck* (Paris: Félix Alcan, 1900) and *La guerre de 1870: causes et responsabilités* (Paris: Plon-Nourrit, 1910).
13. Eugène-Melchior, vicomte de Vogüé, "Impressions d'Allemagne," *Pages d'histoire* (Paris: Armand Colin, 1902), pp. 35–36.
14. Daniel Madelénat, "*Sueur de sang* et les récits de la guerre de 1870," in Pierre Glaudes and Michel Malicet, eds., "Léon Bloy et la guerre de 1870 (autour de *Sueur de sang*)," *La Revue des lettres modernes* (1989), pp. 19–20. Madelénat refers to the "hypermédiatization" surrounding the war, a result of direct reporting and the spectacularization of combat.
15. Paul Déroulède, *1870: Feuilles de route* (Paris: Librairie Félix Juven, 1907).
16. Paul Déroulède, *Chants du soldat: marches et sonneries* (Paris: Calmann-Lévy, 1884).
17. G. Espé de Metz, *70, Cinq tableaux de la guerre* (Paris: L. Fournier, 1911), pp. 73–75.
18. See Jacques Droz, *Les relations franco-allemandes intellectuelles de 1871 à 1914* (Paris: Centre de Documentation Universitaire, 1966), p. 10.
19. Christian Amalvi, "La défaite 'mode d'emploi': Recherches sur l'utilisation rétrospective du passé dans les rapports franco-allemands en France entre 1870 et 1914," in Philippe Levillain and Rainer Riemenschneider, eds., *La guerre de 1870/71 et ses conséquences: actes du XXe Colloque historique franco-allemand* (Bonn: Bouvier, 1990), pp. 451–455.
20. Alfred Fouillée, *Esquisse psychologique*, pp. 97–98.
21. Georges Blondel, *L'essor industriel et commercial du peuple allemand*, 3rd ed. (Paris: L. Larose, 1900), pp. 72–73.
22. Legendre railed against atavistic Prussian militarism, noting that "the power which, in the middle ages, was aimed against eastern barbarism remained armed to maintain

barbarism in the west." Maurice Legendre, *La guerre prochaine et la mission de la France* (Paris: Marcel Riviere, 1913), pp. 91–92.

23. An exception was Bavaria, which, as one French observer noted, refused to celebrate the anniversary of its effective end as an independent state. See Henri de Noussanne, *Le véritable Guillaume II* (Paris: Soc. d'éditions et de publications, 1904), p. 204.

24. See, for example, Gustav Hocker, *1870 und 1871: Zwei Jahre deutschen Heldenthums* (Glogau: C. Flemming, 1906); Oskar Höcker, *Der Nationalkrieg gegen Frankreich in den Jahren 1870 und 1871: Ehrentage aus Deutschlands neuester Geschichte*, 8th ed. (Leipzig: O. Spamer, 1900); Julius von Pflugk-Harttung, *The Franco-German War, 1870–1871* (London: S. Sonnenschein, 1900); Friedrich Regensberg, *1870/71: Der deutsch-französische Krieg* (Stuttgart: Franckh, 1907); Karl Stählin, *Der Deutsch-Französische Krieg 1870/71* (Heidelberg: K. Winters Universitäts Buchhandlung, 1912).

25. Walter Bloem, *Das eiserne Jahr* (Leipzig: Grethlein, 1910); *Volk wider Volk* (1912); *Die Schmiede der Zukunft* (1913). Bloem's German characters demonstrate a strikingly detailed knowledge of the standards and insignia of the entire German army.

26. Karl Bleibtreu, *Die Kommune* (Stuttgart: Carl Krabbe, 1905).

27. Walter Consuelo Langsam, "Nationalism and History in the Prussian Elementary Schools under William II," in Edward Meade Earle, ed., *Nationalism and Internationalism* (New York: Columbia University Press, 1950), p. 259.

28. Paul Rohrbach, *Der deutsche Gedanke in der Welt* (Konigstein im Taunus: K. R. Langewiesche, 1914), p. 105. Rohrbach, however, believed that the German public was mistaken to believe that the next war would be a repeat of 1870–1871, and warned that a future conflict would be far more difficult. See ibid., pp. 217–219.

29. See Holger Afflerbach, *Falkenhayn: Politisches Denken und Handeln im Kaiserreich* (Munich: R. Oldenbourg, 1996), pp. 68–70, and Gerd Krumeich, "Le déclin de la France dans la pensée politique et militaire allemande avant la première guerre mondiale," in Jean-Claude Allain, ed., *La moyenne puissance au XXème siècle: Recherche d'une définition* (Paris: FEDN-IHCC, 1989), pp. 105–107.

30. Felix Victor von Hepke, *Frankreich: Das Heer am Ende des neunzehnten Jahrhunderts* (Berlin: Schall, 1900), pp. 527–528.

31. See Gerd Krumreich, "La puissance militaire française vue d'Allemagne," in Pierre Milza and Raymond Poidevin, eds., *La puissance française à la "Belle Epoque": Mythe ou réalité?* (Paris: Editions Complex, 1992), p. 203.

32. See, for example, the relatively early prediction in Dupuis, *L'évolution militaire*, pp. 86–87.

33. Paul Combes, *La guerre possible* (Paris: Librairie Illustrée, 1906), p. 35. Combes also noted, based on the experience of the Russo-Japanese War, the necessity of seeking cover in future battles and the importance of providing soldiers with the proper tools for digging trenches. See ibid., pp. 111–114.

34. See Commandant de Civrieux, *Le germanisme encerclé* (Paris: H. Charles-Lavauzelle, 1913), p. 5, and Jean d'Is (pseud. of Henri Charles Joseph Miche de Malleray), *Impressions d'un soldat: A travers l'Allemagne* (Paris: Plon-Nourrit, 1914), pp. 9–10.

35. Auguste Antoine Grouard, *France et Allemagne: la guerre éventuelle*, 4th ed. (Paris: Chapelot, 1913), pp. 196–197.

36. André François-Poncet, *Ce que pense la jeunesse allemande* (Paris: G. Oudin, 1913), pp. 42–43, p. 56. François-Poncet later became France's ambassador to Germany during the Nazi period.

37. Arthur Boucher, *La France victorieuse dans la guerre de demain*, rev. ed. (Paris: Berger-Levrault, 1912), pp. v–vi.

38. Paul d'Ivoi and Colonel Royet, *La patrie en danger: histoire de la guerre future* (Paris: Geoffroy, 1905), chap. 23.

39. Legendre, *La guerre prochaine*, pp. 127–128.

40. Georges Aubert, *La folie franco-allemande* (Paris: E. Flammarion, 1914), pp. 61–78.

41. For contemporary accounts, see Victor Bérard, *La France et Guillaume II* (Paris: A. Colin, 1907), pp. 274–275; and Pierre Baudin, *L'empire allemand et l'empereur* (Paris: E. Flammarion,

1911), pp. 50–54. The events at Köpenick inspired a number of plays, the best known of which is Carl Zuckmayer's *Der Hauptmann von Köpenick* (1930), as well as a feature film of the 1950s.

42. A convenient overview can be found in Holger H. Herwig, *The First World War: Germany and Austria-Hungary 1914–1918* (London: Arnold, 1997), pp. 48–50; see also Dieter Storz, "Die Schlacht der Zukunft: Die Vorbereitungen der Armeen Deutschlands and Frankreichs auf den Landkrieg des 20. Jahrhunderts," in Wolfgang Michalka, ed., *Der Erste Weltkrieg: Wirkung, Wahrnehmung, Analyse* (Munich: Piper Verlag, 1994), pp. 252–278. For an interesting description of the welter of contradictions surrounding the Schlieffen Plan and Plan XVII, see L. L. Farrar, *The Short War Illusion: German Policy, Strategy and Domestic Affairs August–December 1914* (Santa Barbara: Clio Press, 1973), pp. 7–9.

43. Stig Förster, "Dreams and Nightmares: German Military Leadership and the Images of Future Warfare, 1871–1914," in Manfred F. Boemeke et al., eds., *Anticipating Total War: The German and American Experiences, 1871–1914* (Cambridge: Cambridge University Press, 1999), pp. 364–365. Förster describes Schlieffen's design as "an old general's dream to prevent a nightmare." See ibid., p. 361.

44. As they did, against all expectations, in May 1940.

45. At least one historian has reached a similar conclusion on the widespread belief in differences in national character and their effects on behavior in combat situations, based on the study of reports by military attachés who observed the annual maneuvers of the French and German armies. See David G. Herrmann, *The Arming of Europe and the Making of the First World War* (Princeton: Princeton University Press, 1996), pp. 79–92.

46. *Frankreichs Ende im Jahre 19?? Ein Zukunftsbild* (Berlin: Verlag Continent, 1912). A French translation appeared the following year.

47. Marieluise Christadler, "Schreckensbild und Vorbild: Die Fremdenlegion in der deutschen Literatur und Propaganda vor 1914," in Helga Abret and Michel Grunewald, eds., *Visions allemandes de la France, 1871–1914* (Bern, New York: P. Lang, 1995), p. 65.

48. Erwin Rosen, *In der Fremdenlegion: Erinnerungen und Eindrücke*, 8th ed. (Stuttgart: R. Lutz, 1914).

49. Ibid., p. 82.

50. Leipzig: Otto Spamer, 1914.

51. Ibid., p. 144.

52. Ibid., p. 153.

53. Hubert Jacques, *L'Allemagne et la Légion* (Paris: Chapelot, 1914), pp. 131–137. Jacques was the war correspondent of *Le Matin* in Morocco. He wished to refute the brutal image of the Legion in Germany, and provided many photographs in his book that purported to show the actual conditions of legionary life. Jacques accused the German consuls in Rabat and Casablanca of running "desertion agencies" that helped Germans (and others) trying to escape from the Legion. See p. 126.

54. A similar antilegionary campaign took place in Germany after World War II, when German legionaries fought in France's wars in Vietnam and Algeria.

55. See Maurice Ajam, *Le problème économique franco-allemand* (Paris: Perrin et Cie., 1914), pp. 126–127 (a German edition appeared the same year). In fact it was French policy not to use legionnaires on the continent.

56. Thomas Raithel, *Das "Wunder" der inneren Einheit: Studien zur deutschen und französischen Öffentlichkeit bei Beginn des Ersten Weltkrieges* (Bonn: Bouvier Verlag, 1996), p. 68.

57. For a general view of the spy mania in France before 1914, see Michael B. Miller, *Shanghai on the Metro: Spies, Intrigue, and the French between the Wars* (Berkeley: University of California Press, 1994), pp. 24–40.

58. See Allan Mitchell, "The Xenophobic Style: French Counterespionage and the Emergence of the Dreyfus Affair," *Journal of Modern History* 52 (September 1980): 414–425.

59. In fact, the intelligence agencies of the two countries were about evenly matched, with the French possessing superior code-breaking agencies. See Holger H. Herwig, "Imperial Germany," in Ernest R. May, ed., *Knowing One's Enemies: Intelligence Assessment*

before the Two World Wars (Princeton: Princeton University Press, 1984), pp. 62–97, and Christopher M. Andrew, "France and the German Menace," ibid., pp. 127–149.

60. Paul Lanoir, *The German Spy System in France* (London: Mills and Boon, n.d. [1915]; originally published in 1908), pp. 101–103. In their novel about the war of the future, Paul d'Ivoi and Colonel Royet put forward the hypothesis that a huge number of German spies had entered France in the wake of the 1900 Exposition, many of them using commercial aliases. See *La patrie en danger*, pp. 252–253.

61. See, for example, Théodore Cahu and Louis Forest, *L'oubli?* (published as a supplement to *L'Illustration*, 29 July 1899–4 November 1899), a novel about Alsace under German rule, in which it is noted that former "Alsatian" farm workers appeared in Prussian uniform after German occupation in 1870.

62. Paris: Nouvelle librairie nationale, 1913.

63. Ibid., "Avant-Propos," p. viii.

64. Ibid., pp. 70–73.

65. Ibid., p. 130.

66. See, for example, "Un 'Zeppelin' en France," *Le Temps*, 5 April 1913.

67. Emile Berrubé, *Flottes aériennes en France et en Allemagne: aéroplanes et ballons de guerre* (Paris: Berger-Levrault, 1910), pp. 1–6.

68. Sommerfeld, *Frankreichs Ende*, pp. 62–65.

69. It is tempting to make generalizations regarding each nation's preferred aircraft. The airplane was operated by a single pilot, while a zeppelin required a crew and was more of a team effort. The zeppelin may have had a special appeal for Wilhelmine Germany, with its cult of the grandiose and its super-masculine values. Whatever the case, in spite of the initial French lead, the Germans quickly caught up in airplane production after the outbreak of the war. See Herrmann, *The Arming of Europe*, pp. 138–146.

70. Victor Klemperer, *Curriculum Vitae: Jugend um 1900* (Berlin: Siedler Verlag, 1989), vol. 1, pp. 335–336.

71. Ernest Raynaud, "A un soldat allemand," *Les deux Allemagnes: poèmes* (Paris: Mercure de France, 1914), pp. 94–97.

72. "Der Störenfried," *Kölnische Zeitung* (12 March 1913).

Chapter Three

PRODUCTION AND REPRODUCTION: ECONOMY, FERTILITY, AND CONSUMPTION

A people whose men don't want to be soldiers, and whose women refuse
to have children, is a people benumbed in its vitality; it is fated to be
dominated by a younger and fresher race. Think of Greece and the Roman
empire! It is a law of history that the elder societies shall cede their place
to the younger, and this is the condition of the perpetual regeneration of
humanity. Later our turn will come, and the ferocious rule will apply to
us; then the reign of the Asiatics will begin, perhaps of the blacks, who
can tell?

Alfred Kerr, interview with Georges Bourdon[1]

The years following the turn of the century were ones of extraordinarily
rapid economic and social change in France and Germany. Many in both
countries viewed this as an exhilarating time of new opportunities with the
possibility of improvement for the broad mass of the people. However, the
negative aspects of this new world were difficult to overlook. In particular,
certain problems associated with industrial growth and urban expansion,
such as tuberculosis, venereal disease, alcoholism, overcrowded housing,
and an increase in the number of children born to unwed mothers, contributed to a growing fear among the educated classes that society was
running off track. Such troubling domestic developments coincided with a
gradual heightening of international tensions. All of these phenomena
influenced the ways in which French and Germans viewed each other during this period. The focus on negative aspects of society on the opposite
side of the Vosges provided much-needed assurance that conditions on
one's own side were not as bad as they might seem. The same problems
may have been just as prevalent in the observer's country, but one could
quietly ignore the evidence. It was much easier to criticize the neighbor's
slovenly habits than to do one's own housekeeping.

Notes for this chapter begin on page 66.

Two central factors in Franco-German relations, and in the European balance of power generally, after 1870 were the phenomenal growth of Germany's population and the corresponding expansion of the German economy. Germany underwent a wrenching transformation from a primarily agricultural to a primarily industrial economy in the span of a few decades, with a particularly accelerated pace after the mid 1890s. The emergence of a global industrial power in central Europe could not fail to have important consequences for European power politics. While German industrial expansion proceeded at a seemingly exponential pace, French growth was slower. Formerly second among the industrial nations in production, by the turn of the century France had fallen to fourth place, behind Britain, Germany, and the United States respectively. Such a trend clearly presented worrisome long-term consequences. However, because of its more modest growth, France also experienced fewer of the social upheavals and dislocations associated with the rapid industrial growth of Germany.[2]

The change in the demographic and economic balance between the two countries, which on both sides of the Vosges appeared to correspond to the transformed balance of power in the international arena in the wake of 1870, was a source of pride to many Germans and of deep concern to many French. Rates of population increase and rates of industrial growth were often conflated, and far-reaching social, cultural, and moral conclusions were drawn from statistics of what people and machines produced. The attempt to explain the growth of the German economy and the relative stagnation of its French counterpart gave rise to a number of ill-founded generalizations about family life, sexual relations, education, working habits, leisure activities, and character traits extracted from economic and demographic observations. Many of these observations were value judgements, not based on serious empirical inquiry, that nonetheless became widely accepted as truths about the other nation. Underlying these beliefs was an implicit assumption that the cultural norms of a society reflected its material conditions, and that to know the latter was the way to understand the former. Production and reproduction formed the twin poles of a Darwinian axis along which one could search for signs of social pathology, moral debasement, decadence, depravity, and political anarchy, or by contrast stability, rectitude, growth, health, and respect for authority. Observations of society in the opposite country ranged from cautious, appreciative, balanced evaluations to the crudest caricatures of social traits. However, simplistic generalizations held wider appeal for a larger public than informed observation, and stereotyping of national character went in tandem with the increasing tensions in international relations before 1914. The interpretation of complex social and economic phenomena as "virtues" or "vices" in the comparative moral balance between the two nations clearly depended on which side of the frontier one stood, and the stakes riding on the outcome of the game appeared to be huge.

Production

A clear imbalance existed between the numbers of French publications about the German economy and of German works about the economic development of France, there being more French writers on the rising German colossus than German writers on French methods. It was generally conceded by French authors, both hostile and admiring, that the Germans were at the cutting edge of technological innovation, organizational efficiency, vocational training, and the like, particularly in newer industries such as chemicals and electricity. Most accounts of the French economy by German experts were technical in nature, devoted to those branches of industry in which France excelled, and intended for a limited audience wishing to profit from French expertise. Most German writers agreed with their French counterparts that France held the advantage in matters of taste, design, and aesthetics. However, such superiority was cold comfort to French leaders with an eye on the future prospects of French industry. The French might produce better goods for the luxury market, but the Germans seemed to dominate in the production of just about everything else, both quantitatively and qualitatively.[3]

At the heart of French and German evaluations of German industrial expansion was a basic philosophical disagreement as to what economic criteria constituted "success." The most fundamental difference was (and, for many, remains) the dichotomy between the continuing creation of new wealth and the achievement of social stability through a healthy balance of work and leisure. German industrial expansion was clearly beneficial in terms of increasing production and bringing a higher standard of living, but it was also accompanied by undesirable social dislocation. The greater French emphasis on individual fulfillment in the spheres of everyday life outside of work clearly had its attractions, but its economic concomitant was a growth rate lagging well behind that of Germany. Both countries grappled with the problems common to all industrial societies. However, both French and German commentators tended to agree that France faced the more serious challenges. In the absence of a major re-evaluation of French attitudes about work and leisure, the long-term prospects for France appeared bleak.[4] Many German observers criticized the French for lacking entrepreneurial spirit and failing to prepare themselves to compete in the export market (not least by the acquisition of foreign languages), while the French criticized the single-mindedness of the German work ethic, which appeared to many to be an unholy twin of the soulless American capitalist ethos.

As far back as 1877, the popular science fiction writer Jules Verne had published an enduring nightmare vision of German industrialism in what proved to be one of his most popular novels, *The 500 Millions of the Begum*. This work presents as representatives of the two countries the characters of the French professor Sarrasin and the German professor Schultz, both heirs to the fortune of a recently deceased Oriental potentate. The two professors decide to use their newfound wealth in order to build utopian societies in far-off Washington State. Sarrasin's ideal city is Frankville, a place where French ideals of liberty, equality, and fraternity achieve their fruition. Schultz, on the other hand, establishes a counter-utopia in Stahlstadt, an industrial and technological nightmare that soon becomes the largest cannon foundry in the western hemisphere. Stahlstadt, as one might expect, is organized around a tyrannical division of labor, directed from a central "bull tower" reminiscent of early nineteenth-century prison designs. As one historian has noted, Schultz hints at Krupp, a figure whose name was synonymous in France with militarism.[5] Addicted to sausages, sauerkraut, and beer, Schultz is a crude caricature of a German industrial robber baron, a Teutonic Hephaestus toiling at his forge, determined to destroy his French rival with hideous secret weapons. However, in the end Schultz is overcome and French idealism triumphs over German materialism.

Verne's disturbing vision of the German industrial nemesis maintained a pervasive hold on the French imagination. The uneasiness with which French observers viewed developments across the Rhine often translated into attacks on the dehumanizing effects of technological innovation and industrial and urban expansion. The demonization of the German paradigm made it possible to argue that France was spared many of the evil consequences of rapid economic growth by its more moderate pace of development—to present a negative structural phenomenon, the relative stagnation of the French economy, as a positive, deliberate policy choice. Nevertheless, as Hartmut Kaelble has demonstrated, in spite of their apparent lead German observers could project the fears inspired by their own modernization and industrialization onto France, perceived as the hotbed of radical socialism and anarchism, thereby exorcizing the demon of political modernism that many feared could disrupt German society.[6] Clearly, each country wished to enjoy the benefits of modernization while avoiding what each perceived as its least desirable aspects. Hence, each projected its greatest fears onto the other.

Just about every observer of the economic scene in France and Germany after 1890 was convinced that the German economy was dynamic, while the French economy was relatively stagnant. Self-appointed experts extrapolated broad generalizations about national character and work habits from this simple fact. Many German commentators assumed that the virtues of application and diligence were simply lacking among the French. The economic historian Werner Sombart was not alone in believing that the typical Frenchman was temperamentally unsuited to take part in entrepreneurial activity, preferring the security of a safe post as a government functionary or of a business narrow in scope and ambition, with early retirement as an ultimate goal.[7] Whatever work was done followed a much slower pace than that to which Germans were accustomed. A German entrepreneur complained to the travel writer Jules Huret of the impossibility of doing business in Paris, with its interminable lunches and superfluity of conversation.[8] Such opinions were widespread in Germany during this period. However, they also found some echo among French experts who hoped to reform the French economy along German lines. The economist Maurice Ajam compared labor in France and Germany, finding that French workers were often more skilled, but that the better German organization and technology of mass production gave a decisive edge to the Germans.[9] Ajam also noted that German entrepreneurs tended to put off retirement longer than their French counterparts, and that more of them had the additional spur of large families.[10] The economist Georges Blondel, who was well acquainted with economic conditions in Germany, likewise praised the superiority of German education and even lauded German methods of parenting. In particular, he admired the career choices German parents made for their children, which were often in spheres of entrepreneurial activity rather than the safer realms of government service or the liberal professions.[11] The historian Henri Lichtenberger noted the importance of associations in the German economy, explaining that they not only made economic organization easier and more effective, but also met the need felt by Germans to see themselves as part of a vast enterprise.[12] By contrast, the vaunted individualism of the French seemed to be a drawback to the organization of large-scale economic activity. The economist Louis Bruneau concluded that a mutual arrangement, advantageous to both countries, was the most desirable course of action. Germany faced a critical shortage of coal and iron, which France possessed in abundance and could trade for German manufactures.[13] The old possibility of alliance, mooted by the likes of Renan on the cultural plane, thus occasionally appeared in the economic realm as well. However, most French writers on the subject feared that France would be very much the junior partner in such an arrangement and ran the risk of becoming a mere appendage to the German behemoth.

One of the most enthusiastic French admirers of German economic performance was the engineer Victor Cambon, who published two books about his observations in Germany. Cambon waxed rhapsodic about German education, research, organization, and economic acumen. He considered the Germans to excel above all others in the rational and systematic application of scientific knowledge.[14] Cambon praised the dynamism of German industrialists, who did not remain satisfied with current products but constantly strove to produce new ones; he also admired the readiness of these knights of industry to take substantial risks.[15] Above all, Cambon was struck by the German desire for constant learning and study, something he perceived as sorely lacking among his French compatriots. When he toured the Borsig locomotive factory in Berlin and examined the visitors' logbook, he discovered that only a handful of French visitors had bothered to make the trip to this state-of-the-art facility.[16] The stay-at-home French were clearly ill-prepared to observe the latest developments abroad. Cambon's second book, published in 1914, is more somber in tone even while expressing admiration for the further economic developments of the intervening four years. Clearly, France had an ever more formidable opponent to face, whether in peaceful economic competition or war, and Cambon realized that it was becoming increasingly difficult for France to make good its deficit.[17]

Not all French accounts of the emerging giant across the Vosges were so admiring of German capitalism. Pierre Baudin offered an extensive critique of the "German conquest" that threatened to overwhelm France without the use of military means.[18] Bertrand Andrillon, a captain in the French army, likewise noted that German firms were able to compete more effectively with their French rivals even within France, and predicted that German economic expansion would ultimately lead to war.[19] Paul Pilant, in his book on "the German peril," related instances of alleged German industrial espionage, whereby German industry hoped to profit from French research.[20] Other French authors, wishing to emphasize France's advantages rather than focus on the more rapid growth of the German economy, preferred to compare lifestyles in France and Germany, for here the French appeared to have an edge. In this comparison the teleological differences between the two nations concerning the ultimate purpose of all human activity came to the fore. While some French observers believed that much could be learned from the German example, few advocated a wholesale Germanization of French economy and society. Most considered the German emphasis on work as the path to fulfillment to be excessive and antithetical to the French spirit, and believed that the cultivation of other spheres—romantic, familial, artistic, intellectual, social—was equally important. Many critics, and not just in France, viewed the rising tide of industrialization as literally "dispiriting," subordinating all other pursuits to a crude materialism and stunting individual development. One writer went so far as to describe German, like American, industrial expansion as an "erreur de jeunesse," lacking the prudence and calm of French growth.[21] Lucien Hubert mourned the death of the sentimental, dreamy Germany of old and feared the danger of Germany becoming Americanized, with no time left for its old intellectual pursuits. Hubert hoped that German economic success might ultimately bring the desire for some of the comforts that the French took for granted and for which they were so harshly criticized in Germany.[22] Georges Blondel agreed, for he considered the life of the spirit to be half-dead in Germany and temporarily surviving in France only because of the lag in industrial expansion.[23] In a later book, Blondel noted that the prosperity brought about by industrialization had nevertheless failed to raise the intellectual and moral level of the masses, a failure that could only bear evil fruit in the future.[24] Georges Bourdon, however, believed that the Germans had retained their old virtues, but feared the possible results of advancing industrialization and the combination of traditional German traits with the new materialist urge. This new synthesis resulted in a Germany whose future actions were difficult to predict: "She is importunate of enjoyments and pleasure, devoured by that insatiable appetite which prosperity and riches, when they come, give to a people to whom victory has long been denied, and with it all she remains cautious, energetic, obstinate, and patient. When such a people becomes ambitious and avows itself so, there is no saying to what lengths its ambition may lead."[25]

The conduct of work itself further accentuated differences in lifestyle. Many French observers considered the organization of production in Germany to be dehumanizing both in working conditions and in the inferior quality of manufactured goods. Jules Huret considered German methods a true reflection of the heavy and pedantic German soul, which he contrasted with the lively intelligence of the French.[26] Paul Valéry wrote an effective critique of the "methodical conquest" of humanity by consumer society as represented by modern Germany. The tone of his words is strikingly familiar even today:

> This action is not, like ours, accidental. It is well-informed. All branches of knowledge are put at its service. It is guided by a subtle psychology, and for that reason it does better than simply impose itself: it makes itself desired. It is necessary that the customer of Germany render his blessing on the German merchant, and even on German traits. Indeed, this customer must become a friend, a disseminator—a calculation that is of a profound elegance. Now, this customer is well-known. This client, who believes himself free, living in innocence, is studied without his knowing it, without his being touched. He is classified, defined according to his city, his province, his country. They know what he eats, what he drinks, what he smokes, and how he pays. They meditate on his wants. In Hamburg or Nuremberg, someone has perhaps plotted the graphs that represent the exploitation of his smallest cravings, of his slightest needs. He would see himself—he who sees himself as living so personally, so intimately—lumped together there with thousands of other personalities who *prefer* the same liquor, the same fabric as he does. Because over there they know more about his own country than he knows himself. They know better than he the most trivial details of his own existence, what he needs to live, and what he needs to provide a little amusement in his life. They know his vanity, that he dreams of objects of luxury, and that he finds them too expensive. They will make him anything necessary—champagne from potatoes, perfume from whatever. The customer has no idea how many chemists are thinking about him. They will make for him exactly what satisfies his purse, his desire, and his habits at the same time, and they will produce for him something of a perfect degree of mediocrity. It is by a servile obedience to his complex desire that they get their hands on him.[27]

Valéry saw the age of genius during which France had reigned supreme giving way to a well-organized German mediocrity in which the most mechanical qualities, such as patience and attention to detail, take priority over true genius and creativity.[28] However, his brilliant analysis is less a description of specific German conditions than an attack on modern consumer society, whose most conspicuous representative for so many French people was Germany.

Many perturbed French writers asked themselves what the results of all this frantic activity would be. Blondel, probably the best-informed French observer of the German economy, thought that the logic of industrial development offered Germany only two alternatives. One was to follow the British model and embark on a road of global conquest; the other, to follow the policy of self-provision suggested by the nineteenth-century economist Friedrich List and remove itself entirely from the vagaries of the world market by supplying virtually all of its own needs. It does not seem to have occurred to Blondel that the one alternative did not necessarily exclude the other. During the period under examination, however, most of the French public became convinced that Germany had settled on the first course and was embarking on an expansionist path.

There was one area of economic activity where the Germans had to recognize that France held a lead, and this was in the realm of finance. The traditional thriftiness of the French peasant, combined with the relatively low demand for capital domestically due to the slower growth rate of French industry, meant that France had a great deal of capital liquidity, and Parisian banks made loans all over the globe. French financial strength was a matter of great prestige for France, or so it was often portrayed to the French public. Germany, by contrast, was chronically short of fluid capital. Given this context, international investment opportunities could sometimes entail discord between the two countries. The Berlin-to-Baghdad Railway, a German-inspired project in the Ottoman Empire that was largely financed by French and British capital, is perhaps the best-known example. Opinion in both countries differed as to how far the French government was willing to use capital as a weapon in relations with Germany. One German authority thought that the recall of French loans to Germany after the Agadir crisis helped to contribute to the economic slump of 1912.[29] However, there were limits to the influence France could wield with international loans. French loans sometimes served to finance the purchase of German industrial goods, including armaments, as was the case in Turkey in the years just before the Balkan Wars.[30] Nevertheless, most French writers on the subject considered France's financial assets to be a trump card in Franco-German relations. Many would have agreed with Henry Gaston's assertion that the French economy rested on a bed of gold, while that of Germany was built on sand.[31]

In spite of such optimistic evaluations, France clearly faced difficult choices if it wished to counter the German economic and military threat. The alternative was to allow the German juggernaut to become the unchallenged economic power on the continent. France would clearly have to undertake major reforms even to achieve parity with its arch-rival. Unfortunately for France, its problems were not confined to the realm of economic productivity.

Reproduction

The issue of economic growth was closely linked to that of population increase. Many authors of the period in both countries linked fertility to productivity and consumption, demonstrating that more births meant more workers and also a larger domestic market for home-produced goods. In the economic and demographic spheres Germany clearly seemed to hold the lead, and many French experts worried about the long-term consequences of France's slow population growth. It did not become clear for several decades that the French case was the precursor of a general European—indeed global—trend toward decreasing demographic expansion. However, at the beginning of the twentieth century it appeared that France was exceptional in its declining fertility, and few on either side of the frontier doubted that this was an undesirable development given the prevailing Social Darwinist view of international affairs. As one prominent German observer noted in 1914, if current trends continued Germany's population would be twice that of France at some point between 1925 and 1930.[32]

The topics of sex, gender relations, and family life frequently appear in accounts of the opposite country published in France and Germany during this period. The equation of production and reproduction, frequently encountered in a wide array of publications before World War I, was admirably suited to the prevailing Darwinist world view, and it helped to sell books. However, there were reasons other than prurience for focusing on sexual mores. It was widely assumed that private life influenced public affairs, indeed that the strength and stability of the body politic was in direct proportion to the "health" of the individuals who composed it. Attention focused on gender relations and the family, perhaps because it was these very institutions seemed most under threat from the modern society that was in the process of emerging in both countries.[33]

German critiques of French sexual relations and family life tended to use the low French birth rate as a point of departure from which to draw larger conclusions about the French family. The two-child family was already the norm in France by the turn of the century, while the average German family size was exceeded only by the less developed regions of eastern and southeastern Europe.[34] Paul Rohrbach, a well-known prophet of German *Weltpolitik*, compared the lower French birth rate to that of the patrician classes in imperial Rome, and considered the French case the greater danger because in France the smaller family was common to *all* classes.[35] The German critic Alfred Kerr, in an interview with the journalist Georges Bourdon, criticized French women for their apparent reluctance to bear more children. Kerr stated that France had reached a level of culture that placed too high an emphasis on individual fulfillment and too little on military discipline. Kerr's implication that French culture was somehow "feminized" reflected convictions that were deeply rooted among his German contemporaries.[36] One dissenting voice in the matter of French birth rates was the political scientist Hermann Fernau. Fernau demonstrated that the birth rate in the more enlightened German cities was comparable to that of France, and he argued that it was precisely the poorest and most religious elements of the population that had the most children.[37] Fernau also noted that the ultimate rationale for higher birth rates was to provide more soldiers for future wars.[38] Unfortunately, Fernau's sensible arguments did not reach a wide audience.

France's alleged "decadence" and its effects on France's economic capacity and military preparedness were apparently obsessive themes among German commentators of these years. Of course, more than mere scientific curiosity lay behind much of the interest in this topic. Few German visitors to Paris just after the turn of the century wasted the opportunity to tour Montmartre to view the latest manifestations of the moral decline of French civilization.[39] Guides to nighttime Paris in German or English were easily available from Parisian street hawkers, with addresses of the latest fashionable dens of iniquity. One German guide book of the period provided its own list, but noted that, as such information changed from year to year, it was best for the visitor to inquire at his hotel.[40] The conflation of Montmartre with the whole of France was not confined to German tourists, but seems to have had a particularly strong hold on the German imagination. However, one German writer went against the trend when he noted that many of the "priestesses of Venus" in Montmartre were themselves German, and that the "international Aphrodite cult" of Paris had no more practitioners than that of London, Vienna, Berlin, or Budapest, and had nothing to do with national character or the mentality of the race.[41] The great Alsatian caricaturist Hansi described the adventures of his antihero Professor Knatschke and his companion, the *Rechnungsrat* Lempke, as they explore Paris and write fatuous comments in their notebooks. The hapless academic is startled to witness the apparent transformation of an innocent schoolgirl into a prostitute, and earnestly draws dire conclusions about the state of French society (fig. 2).[42]

Most Germans of the period accepted it as a given that the Frenchman was far more preoccupied with women than his German counterpart, and many of their French contemporaries would probably have agreed. Theodor Wolff, Paris correspondent (and later editor) of the *Berliner Tageblatt*, noted in his published journal of his years in the French capital that five hundred thousand Parisians had turned out to watch a young Australian woman swim the length of the Seine—less out of admiration for her athletic prowess than for appreciation of the female form.[43] French observers of Germany, by contrast, tended to see Germans as somewhat inept in matters of the heart. The travel writer Jules Huret claimed that while the French are tolerant toward adolescents and their love affairs, the Germans (like the English and Americans) are mortified by youthful amours, reserving greater indulgence for heavy drinking.[44] In her delightful memoir, *Au*

Une fillette à peine sortie
de l'école...

Je vis la fillette dont il a été question plus haut, laquelle
assise à une table, avec un apache...

FIGURE 2: Professor Knatschke and his companion witness the apparent transformation of an innocent Parisian schoolgirl into a prostitute. (Hansi, *Professeur Knatschké: œuvres choisies du Grand Savant Allemand et de sa fille Elsa*. Paris: H. Floury, 1912, pp. 41, 44)

pair: une Française en Allemagne, the young author Henriette Celarié recalled a summer spent with a noble Prussian family in Brandenburg. The son, Wilhelm, was enamored of her and even proposed marriage. Initially, the young French woman felt some attraction for the young German nobleman. However, whatever interest Celarié might have had in such a match rapidly evaporated when her would-be fiancé beat a peasant for theft in full view of his beloved.[45] Celarié also noted disapprovingly that German men generally ignored their wives, valuing in them a good cook far more than a pleasant conversationalist.[46]

Discussions touching on matters of pregnancy and childbirth tended to reveal very different attitudes toward the subject in both countries. In a book that was originally published in 1878 and remained popular in the following decades, the Francophile author Karl Hillebrand noted with admiration the ability of French women to discuss pregnancy without resorting to euphemisms to describe their condition.[47] Birth control and abortion aroused strong emotions in both countries, but there was a predominant, and accurate, impression that they were more common in

France. Condoms were popularly referred to in Germany as "Pariser," while the abortionist or *faiseuse d'anges* was widely supposed to be thriving in France where, many Germans believed, more frivolous attitudes toward childbearing and childrearing reigned.[48] This conviction was not confined to the German side of the frontier. The economist Georges Aubert thought that an effective way to resist Germany would be to declare war on French abortionists, who threatened to undermine France's preparedness for war.[49] Nevertheless, other French observers pointed out that while Germany had a higher birth rate, its mortality rates of infants and childbearing women were among the highest in western Europe, and approached those of some Balkan countries.[50] The Alsatian writers Jeanne and Frédéric Régamey noted in their extremely hostile *L'Allemagne ennemie* that statistics on wife abandonment, divorce, and illegitimacy belied German claims of superior domestic virtue.[51] In addition, they noted the effects of heavy alcohol consumption by German men and women, which contributed to the neglect of children by parents.[52] Clearly, arguments about which nation had healthier families might draw on "scientific" data but were nonetheless largely fanciful (fig. 3).

The personifications of France and Germany in caricature provide clues to many of the assumptions prevalent in each country about the other. In both countries, France was usually pictured as a woman, a variation on Marianne, occasionally as a French soldier. Germany, by contrast, was usually pictured as a man, either the kaiser or a German soldier, and only occasionally as the female warrior Germania, who had not achieved the level of popularity in Germany as had Marianne in France.[53] (The conventional German figure of *der deutsche Michel*, dim-witted but honest, does not seem to appear in French accounts.) German caricatures of Marianne could occasionally be quite crude, implying sexual license, hysteria, or insane jealousy. Caricatures of Germany in France tended more to the buffoonish or ridiculous, with peculiarities such as Wilhelm II's moustache making for endless delight. Nevertheless, the choice of gender in each case does not seem to have been entirely accidental. The equation of France with woman, and the portrayal of Frenchmen as effeminate, revealed a deep-seated contempt for France in the hyper-masculine world of Wilhelmine Germany. Metaphors of exhaustion and depletion reinforced a general notion of French impotence. At the same time, the French were clearly puzzled, amused, and occasionally alarmed by the gauche machismo of German military and diplomatic circles, and the evident eagerness with which other German social groups imitated their betters' militant maleness (figs. 4 and 5).

Some French observers, at least, detected something further in all this male posturing. While German observers could display a prurient interest in the Parisian demi-monde, there was one kind of pleasure the French dubbed "the German vice." Homosexuality was probably at least as common in Paris as in Berlin, but Berlin was already cast in the role of Sodom to the Parisian Babylon.[54] There had been a number of works by French

FIGURE 3: *Pariser Seufzer:* "Have you heard that in Germany they've found a way to get babies without men?" "*Mon dieu,* and we don't even get them *with* men!" (*Simplicissimus,* 8 July 1912)

FRANCE ET RUSSIE
(*Ulk*, 21 janvier 1898)

FIGURE 4: France and Russia. A jealous Marianne prepares to throw vitriol on a demure Germania being courted by Russia. (*Ulk*, 21 January 1898; reproduced in John Grand-Carteret, *L'Affaire Dreyfus et l'image*. Paris: Ernest Flammarion, 1899)

authors on the gay subculture of Berlin during the nineteenth century.[55] However, a celebrated scandal focused renewed attention on an underworld that was already long established. Prince Philipp zu Eulenburg-Hertefeld was a member of the entourage of Wilhelm II and one of the kaiser's closest friends. In 1907 he was "outed" in a famous series of articles by Maximilian Harden, the combative editor of *Die Zukunft*, aided by political opponents of Eulenburg.[56] The Eulenburg affair resulted in the prince's disgrace and caused persistent rumors to circulate concerning the imperial entourage, including the kaiser himself. Several books devoted to the affair and the subject of homosexuality in Germany appeared in France in 1907–1908. Some French observers considered the very term "homosexual" itself

In Nancy
„Allons, gamins! – De la patrie
La jour de gloire est arrivé!"

FIGURE 5: Marianne leads the mob against the German tourists at Nancy.
"Follow me! Our country's day of glory has arrived!" *Kladderadatsch* 66 (27 April 1913)

to be an odd German neologism, popularized by writers such as the well-known sexologist Magnus Hirschfeld.[57] One study of homosexuality in Germany noted that, in spite of the severe penalties against sexual relations between men, "platonic" love was somewhat more open in Germany, and, if probably no more prevalent than in France or other European countries, more in keeping with the Teutonic than the Latin soul.[58] It found accordingly that almost all homosexuals were Wagnerians![59] And it concluded that the decadence of the German aristocracy produced a disproportionate number of "degenerates," which went far toward explaining the evidently large proportion of homosexuals in the Prussian officer corps.[60]

The French playwright Oscar Méténier visited Berlin for the opening of his stage version of Maupassant's *Boule de suif* in 1908 and published a remarkable account of his experiences. In the course of his stay, Méténier was introduced by a French friend resident in the city to the relatively open world of Berlin gay society, which he referred to as "this Church of a new type."[61] He visited gay clubs and attended a transvestite ball, where he made the acquaintance of Magnus Hirschfeld. Méténier appeared to be surprised by the courtesy and good behavior of the participants at these gatherings. Nevertheless, he could not resist reflecting on the "inverts," as he called them, as the inevitable result of a strict German morality, which inculcated distrust of and disgust for women.[62] Méténier observed that homosexuality appeared to be especially prevalent among the German officer caste, members of which appeared in large numbers at the functions he witnessed and in the well-known cruising grounds of the Tiergarten in Berlin. Méténier was particularly struck by the prevalence of homosexuality among the "respectable" elements of Berlin society.

The demographic difference between France and Germany boiled down to a simple phenomenon: there were more German babies than French babies. There was no serious policy to increase French birth rates, and it was not yet clear that German births would decrease over the long term. In a world dominated by notions of the struggle for existence, Germany seemed to be predominating in the battle of births. However, as time was to prove, numbers did not dictate the course of events, nor did they guarantee a secure future.

Consumption

The private life of the opposite nation could give rise to endless speculation on national character. If work habits, gender relations, and sexual proclivities seemed to provide a key to understanding a nation, then culinary customs and styles of alcohol consumption could be equally revealing. In the realm of the table, as even most cultivated Germans admitted, the French enjoyed a clear advantage. French cuisine had provided the model for most of Europe for centuries, and many Germans were passionate admirers of French food and wine. French observations regarding the eating habits of the Germans, by contrast, could be savage. Many French appeared to be convinced that the average citizen of Germany was an amalgam of beer, sauerkraut, and bad manners. In spite of this, some French writers who bothered to cross the frontier were pleasantly surprised by the fare they found in the better German eating establishments.

Most French observers seemed to believe that Germans consumed enormous amounts of disgusting food, washed down with endless draughts of beer, in surroundings that were correspondingly repellent to the sensitive Gallic soul. Jules Huret, in the volume of his travel work devoted to

Bavaria, described a nightmare evening spent at the Hofbräuhaus in Munich, and catalogued the bewildering variety of appalling *Wurst* one could order.[63] A French officer traveling in Germany was astonished at the huge quantities of food he saw being eaten in a beer garden by the solid burghers of Eisenach, in contrast to the more delicate fare generally available in France.[64] However, even in Germany an occasional island of *haute cuisine* offered shelter from the sea of culinary barbarism. Oscar Méténier expressed his delight with the finer restaurants of Berlin, which, it appears, offered a more cultivated fare than the typical German establishment.[65] However, most polite French travelers simply failed to comment on the cuisine they encountered in Germany, apparently accepting with grace one of the inevitable hardships of traveling outside France.

Differences in taste concerning the preparation of food might make for amusing anecdotes, but the topic of alcohol, and particularly of its abuse, raised more sensitive issues. Contrasting styles of alcohol consumption and beliefs concerning the prevalence of alcoholism contributed heavily to the image of the opposite nation in each country. Some observers pointed out that the social ills caused by alcoholism were equally present in both France and Germany.[66] However, it was generally accepted, even by many Germans, that the average German consumed more alcohol than his French counterpart, legends concerning the prodigious consumption of *absinthe* by the typical Parisian notwithstanding.[67] Some French authors elevated alcohol consumption into the defining characteristic of the German race. The rabidly anti-German Léon Daudet described Germany as the land of chronic intoxication, a state to which the pharmaceutical industry contributed by its creation of new drugs. Daudet thereby associated a social ill with one of the most successful branches of German industry![68] In their novel about a future German invasion of France, the pulp writers Paul d'Ivoi and Colonel Royet described German soldiers drinking huge quantities of champagne and liquor at dinner "with that absence of taste, that gluttony, which is the hallmark of their race."[69]

Some Germans who published accounts of their experiences in France reflected on the differing roles of drink in the social life of the two countries. The prominent National Liberal politician Friedrich Naumann, pondering his observations during travels in France, thought that people who drank wine were more sensitive than beer drinkers, while the travel writer Walther Gensel considered that the drinking that went on in French cafés was a secondary activity to conversation and socializing, in marked contrast to the conduct one generally observed in German beer halls.[70] Some French authors thought they detected a peculiar joylessness in German drinking, which contrasted markedly with the conviviality of its French counterpart. In his collection of poems entitled *The Two Germanies*, the poet Ernest Raynaud devoted one poem, ironically titled *Erholungsort* (health resort), to a melancholy evening in a tavern:

> While the prostitutes prowl around the barracks
> Under the rain, by the light of pale lanterns
> With borrowed smiles masking souls in mourning
> Here a warm glow greets us.
>
> *Prosit!* Voluptuousness breathes on the threshold
> Its eyes sparkle as if intensified by their dark rings;
> The imperial bust proudly presides
> Over your listless games, strange tavern.
>
> A colored chandelier makes things sparkle
> A bouquet of roses withers on the table
> There is singing at the piano; the rings shine brightly.
>
> Drunkenness is well advanced in the animated room.
> Otto von Schmetterling sees his dream around him
> Rising and descending through a cloud of smoke.[71]

Similarly, in their serialized novel set in occupied Metz, Thédore Cahu and Louis Forest portrayed a typical drunken binge of the bored German officers of the garrison:

> With his face plunged into his beer glass, his nose in the liquid, his moustache covered with foam, each man sought, amid vile burps, to pass the idle hours, and when, amidst the longed-for abasement, among the barbarous yells of growing drunkenness, the serving girl circulated with her hands full of glasses, arms rose, wrapped around her waist in indolent embrace, then fell again.
>
> The officers of the garrison had no other pleasure than to keep bad company, to become stupefied amidst the shouts of the breweries, the odor of sausages, the various stenches, and the dense smoke of the porcelain pipes.[72]

Such scenes of public drunkenness were surely not unknown in France as well, and present-day statistics show that rates of alcoholism are similar in France and Germany. Nevertheless, while a naturalist novel such as Emile Zola's *L'assommoir* might clearly portray the evils of alcoholism in France, the perception remained that this particular scourge was a greater social problem in Germany than in France.

Conclusion

A study of the mythologies of private life that French and Germans constructed of each other during this period provides interesting examples of how politics distorted the perception of the ordinary. The formation of absurdly broad theories of national character was often based on extremely limited empirical observation that did not take sufficient account of individual peculiarities. The values used as measuring rods, whether clearly stated or merely implied, were usually assumed to be eternal verities when in fact they too shifted with time and varied tremendously from person to person. Thus, the smallest details of everyday life were fitted into a rigid conceptual framework. It is little wonder then that, in his classic book on French mores, Karl Hillebrand resorted to a familiar accompaniment of German meals in describing the nostalgia typically felt by Germans living in France:

> In such moods a German may well long after "divine rudeness" and steaming *Sauerkraut*, and, even without the terrible catastrophes in which the Celtic lava from time to time comes to the surface, may be ready to give up all the gaiety and refined enjoyment of life for the needy simplicity and honest earnestness of his own country, where, indeed, he never knew what it was "to live like a god in France," but where he now feels that beneath the rough and unsightly shell there lies concealed a sweet and delicate kernel.[73]

Certain everyday aspects of given cultures that are usually taken for granted, such as culinary staples, are so prevalent that their prolonged absence brings an intense yearning that surrounds the missing object with childhood associations. The linking of elevated sentiments of national piety with a bowl of sauerkraut might appear strange at first sight, but Hillebrand knew that the senses of taste and smell are gateways to deepest memory, and doubtless many travelers on both sides of the frontier experienced acute deprivation, dislocation, and nostalgia when faced with unfamiliar customs. Oftentimes such disorientation could contribute to a certain sense of impatience or hostility that the circumstances did not warrant, leading to rash judgements based on insufficient information.

The tendency to view culture as a holistic entity tempted French and Germans to make excessively wide-ranging generalizations about each other based on very slim evidence. The boundaries between various categories of culture and aspects of everyday life were indistinct in the minds of many observers on both sides. Thus, it was extremely difficult for most observers to avoid imposing an *a priori* model of expected behavior accompanied by a well-developed set of images. The notion of national character, while having some foundation in the common history, culture, and material circumstances of a people, is a shifting and evasive wraith. Often the qualities ascribed to a nation as essential and immutable components of its nature are merely passing phases, misunderstood customs, or the peculiarities of a minority. It is far easier to accept exaggerated or distorted notions of national character when direct experience of the nation in question is relatively limited. The large-scale contact between ordinary French and Germans that would have served to temper hostile mythologies and perhaps allay fears did not become possible until after World War II. Failing this kind of interaction, most French and Germans were left to believe the worst of their neighbors and adversaries across the Vosges.

Notes

1. Georges Bourdon, *The German Enigma: Being an Inquiry among the Germans as to What They Think, What They Want, What They Can Do*, trans. by Beatrice Marshall (London: J.M. Dent and Sons, 1914), p. 170.

2. For a good survey of the subject, see Raymond Poidevin, *Les relations économiques et financières entre la France et l'Allemagne de 1898 à 1914* (Paris: Comité pour l'histoire économique et financière de la France, 1969).

3. See Raymond Poidevin, "La peur de la concurrence allemande en France avant 1914," in Johannes Vandenrath et al., *1914: Les psychoses de guerre* (Mont-Saint-Aignan: Publications de l'Université de Rouen, 1985), pp. 77–84.

4. Indeed, the situation seemed further aggravated in the 1920s as a result of France's massive loss of manpower in World War I.

5. Hans T. Siepe, "Die Höhle des Drachen und das Herz der Hölle: Zur Mythologisierung des Ruhrgebiets in der französischen Literatur zwischen 1870 und 1923," in Michel Grunewald and Jochen Schlobach, eds., *Médiations: aspects des relations franco-allemandes du XVIIe siècle à nos jours* (Berne and New York: P. Lang, 1992), vol. 1, p. 309.

6. Hartmut Kaelble, "Die vergessene Gesellschaft im Westen? Das Bild der Deutschen von der französischen Gesellschaft, 1871–1914," *Revue d'Allemagne* 21, no. 2 (April–June, 1989): 181. It is curious to note that no German observer during this period seems to have taken account of the fact that French rural economy and society—stable, conservative, and following a rhythm established by centuries of customary usage—bore a greater resemblance to the ideals of *Blut und Boden* so dear to many German conservatives than did much of Germany itself. Only in the 1930s, just when the French rural economy was in serious crisis, did German writers begin to take serious note of it. See the works by Paul Distelbarth and Karl Tögel.

7. Werner Sombart, *The Quintessence of Capitalism: A Study of the History and Psychology of the Modern Business Man*, trans. by M. Epstein (New York: Howard Fertig, 1967), pp. 136–140; originally published as *Der Bourgeois*, 1913.

8. Jules Huret, *En Allemagne: De Hambourg aux marches de Pologne* (Paris: E. Fasquelle, 1908), p. 230.

9. Maurice Ajam, *Le problème économique franco-allemand* (Paris: Perrin et Cie., 1914), pp. 33–36. A German edition of Ajam's book appeared the same year.

10. Ibid., pp. 115–116.

11. Georges Blondel, *Conférence … sur l'expansion commerciale comparée de la France et de l'Allemagne* (Paris: Librairies-Imprimeries réunies, 1899), pp. 37–39.

12. Henri Lichtenberger, *L'Allemagne moderne: son évolution* (Paris: E. Flammarion, 1912), pp. 388–392.

13. Louis Bruneau, *L'Allemagne en France: enquêtes économiques* (Paris: Plon-Nourrit, 1914), p. 9.

14. Victor Cambon, *L'Allemagne au travail* (Paris: P. Roger, 1910), p. 3.

15. Ibid., p. 45.

16. Ibid., p. 164.

17. Victor Cambon, *Les derniers progrès de l'Allemagne*, 3rd ed. (Paris: P. Roger, 1914).

18. Pierre Baudin, *L'empire allemand et l'empereur* (Paris: E. Flammarion, 1911), pp. 144–155.

19. Bertrand Andrillon, *L'expansion de l'Allemagne: ses causes, ses formes, ses conséquences* (Paris: M. Riviere et cie., 1914), pp. 118–119. Georges Blondel even knew of a German factory that manufactured French tricolor flags and was able to import them into France at a competitive price. Georges Blondel, *L'essor industriel et commercial du peuple allemand*, 3rd ed. (Paris: L. Larose, 1900), p. 221.

20. Paul Pilant, *Le péril allemand* (Paris: Editions et librairie, 1913), pp. 142–144.

21. Henry Gaston, *Où va l'Allemagne: A la faillite? A la guerre? A la révolution?* (Paris: Editions et librairie, 1913), pp. 14–15.

22. Lucien Hubert, *L'effort allemand: l'Allemagne et la France au point de vue économique* (Paris: Félix Alcan, 1911), pp. 227–230.

23. Blondel, *Conférence*, pp. 31–32.

24. Georges Blondel, *Les embarras de l'Allemagne* (Paris: Plon-Nourrit, 1912), p. iii.

25. Georges Bourdon, *The German Enigma*, p. 8.

26. Jules Huret, *En Allemagne: De Hambourg aux marches de Pologne* (Paris: E. Fasquelle, 1908), pp. 215–216.

27. Paul Valéry, "Une conquête méthodique," *Œuvres*, vol. 1 (Paris: Gallimard, 1957), p. 974. The essay first appeared in a British journal in 1897.

28. Ibid., p. 981.

29. Arthur Feiler, *Die Konjunktur-Periode 1907–1913 in Deutschland* (Jena: G. Fischer, 1914), pp. 121–122.

30. Raymond Poidevin, "Weltpolitik allemande et capitaux français 1898–1914," in Imanual Geiss and Bernd Jürgen Wendt, eds., *Deutschland in der Weltpolitik des 19. und 20. Jahrhunderts* (Düsseldorf: Bertelsmann Universitätsverlag, 1974), pp. 242–243.

31. Gaston, *Où va l'Allemagne*, pp. 62–66.

32. Kurt Riezler [under the pseudonym J. J. Ruedorffer], *Die Erforderlichkeit des Unmöglichen* (Munich: G. Muller, 1913), p. 82.

33. For an excellent summary of the French obsession with the declining birth rate before 1914 and the perceived necessity for pro-natalist policies in the face of the German threat, see Michael S. Teitelbaum and Jay M. Winter, *The Fear of Population Decline* (Orlando: Academic Press, 1985), pp. 18–30.

34. See Hartmut Kaelble, *Nachbarn am Rhein: Entfremdung und Annäherung der französischen Gesellschaft seit 1880* (Munich: Beck, 1991), pp. 42–44. Kaelble points out that in our day only certain parts of Asia and Africa have similar birthrates.

35. Paul Rohrbach, *Deutschland unter den Weltvölkern: Materialien zur auswärtigen Politik*, 3rd ed. (Berlin-Schoneberg: Buchverlag der "Hilfe," 1912), p. 207.

36. Georges Bourdon, *The German Enigma*, p. 170.

37. Hermann Fernau, *Die französische Demokratie: Sozialpolitische Studien aus Frankreichs Kulturwerkstatt* (Munich: Duncker & Humblot, 1914), pp. 195–196.

38. Ibid., p. 201.

39. See Fritz Fischer, "Das Bild Frankreichs in Deutschland in den Jahren vor dem Ersten Weltkrieg," *Revue d'Allemagne* IV, no. 3 (July–September 1972): 508–509.

40. L. Teubner, *Eine Woche in Paris* (Berlin: Georg Stilke, 1909), pp. 46–47.

41. Fritz Friedmann, *Deutschland—Frankreich und Kaiser Wilhelm II: Eine Völkerstudie* (Berlin: A. Pulvermacher & Co., 1912), p. 12.

42. Hansi [pseud. of Jean-Jacques Waltz], *Professor Knatschké: œuvres choisies du Grand Savant Allemand et de sa fille Elsa* (Paris: H. Floury, 1912), pp. 40–44.

43. Theodor Wolff, *Pariser Tagebuch* (Munich: Albert Langen, 1908), pp. 198–199.

44. Jules Huret, *En Allemagne: Rhin et Westphalie* (Paris: E. Fasquelle, 1907), p. 99. "Ici, Roméo surpris à son échelle de soie serait poursuivi et hué, Falstaff aurait tout le monde pour lui." Nevertheless, Huret was startled to encounter men and women swimming together "almost naked" at a lake outside Berlin. Jules Huret, *En Allemagne: Berlin* (Paris: E. Fasquelle, 1909), pp. 54–55.

45. Henriette Celarié, *Au pair: une Française en Allemagne* (Paris: Armand Colin, 1911), pp. 48–50.

46. Ibid., p. 24.

47. Karl Hillebrand, *France and the French* (New York: Scribner and Welford, 1881), p. 34.

48. Jorg von Uthmann, *Le diable est-il allemand?: 200 ans de préjugés franco-allemands* (Paris: Denoel, 1984), p. 172.

49. Georges Aubert, *La folie franco-allemande: étude contemporaine* (Paris: E. Flammarion, 1914), p. ix.

50. See Kaelble, *Nachbarn am Rhein*, pp. 35–36.

51. Jeanne and Frédéric Régamey, *L'Allemagne ennemie* (Paris: Albin Michel, 1913), pp. 48–49.

52. Ibid., pp. 59–61.

53. See Lothar Gall, *Germania: Eine deutsche Marianne?* (Bonn: Bouvier Verlag, 1993).

54. John Grand-Carteret, *Derrière "Lui": l'homosexualité en Allemagne* (Paris: E. Bernard, 1908; reprint ed. Paris: Gai-Kitsch-Camp, 1992), pp. 1–2.

55. For a list, see ibid., p. 4.

56. See the relevant chapters on the Eulenburg affair in Isabel Hull, *The Entourage of Kaiser Wilhelm II, 1888–1918* (Cambridge: Cambridge University Press, 1982) and Harry F. Young, *Maximilian Harden, censor Germaniae: The Critic in Opposition from Bismarck to the Rise of Nazism* (The Hague: M. Nijhoff, 1959).

57. Grand-Carteret, *Derrière "Lui,"* p. 4, note 1. A translation of Hirschfeld's *Berlins drittes Geschlecht* (1904) appeared four years later in France: *Les homosexuels de Berlin: le troisième sexe.*

58. Henri de Weindel and F.-P. Fischer, *L'homosexualité en Allemagne: étude documentaire et anecdotique* (Paris: F. Juven, 1908), pp. 5–6.

59. Ibid., p. 111.

60. Ibid., pp. 174–175.

61. Oscar Méténier, *Les Berlinois chez eux: vertus et vices allemands* (Paris: Albin Michel, n.d. [1908]), p. 93.

62. Ibid., pp. 126–127.

63. Jules Huret, *En Allemagne: La Bavière et la Saxe* (Paris: E. Fasquelle, 1911), pp. 39–44.

64. Jean d'Is (pseud. of Henri Charles Joseph Miche de Malleray), *Impressions d'un soldat: A travers l'Allemagne* (Paris: Plon-Nourrit, 1914), pp. 74–75.

65. Méténier, *Les Berlinois chez eux*, pp. 21–23.

66. See, for example, Alfred Fouillée, *Esquisse psychologique des peuples européens*, 5th ed. (Paris: Félix Alcan, 1914), p. 359.

67. Wilhelm Uhde, *Paris: Eine Impression* (Berlin: Bard, Marquardt, 1904), p. 40.

68. Léon Daudet, *L'avant-guerre: études et documents sur l'espionnage juif-allemand en France depuis l'affaire Dreyfus* (Paris: Nouvelle librairie nationale, 1913), p. 83.

69. Paul d'Ivoi and Colonel Royet, *La patrie en danger: histoire de la guerre future* (Paris: Geoffroy, 1905), p. 153.

70. Friedrich Naumann, "Pariser Briefe," *Die Hilfe* 6 (1900), reprinted in *Werke*, vol. 6, *Ästhetische Schriften* (Cologne: Westdeutscher Verlag, 1964), p. 391; Walther Gensel, *Paris: Studien und Eindrücke* (Leipzig: Thomas Weicher, 1900), p. 32.

71. Ernest Raynaud, *Les deux Allemagnes: poèmes* (Paris: Mercure de France, 1914), pp. 81–82.

72. Théodore Cahu and Louis Forest, *L'oubli?* (Published as a supplement to *L'Illustration*, 29 July 1899–4 November 1899): 3.

73. Hillebrand, *France and the French*, p. 105.

Chapter Four

The Elusive Alsatian

The province of Alsace and much of Lorraine, annexed by Germany in the aftermath of the war of 1870–1871, formed the single most divisive issue between the two countries in the decades before World War I. They were one of the root causes, as well as an ever-present reminder, of the Franco-German enmity after 1871. As Georges Ducrocq, a French travel writer of Alsatian origin, described the problem in 1910, the loss of the provinces had left "a poorly healed wound" in the collective French psyche.[1] The French at that time considered this annexation to be an unbearable blow to national pride and French standing among the great powers. Many Germans, by contrast, regarded the same annexation as a return of historically "German" territory, both provinces having been part of the Holy Roman Empire until 1648. In 1871, Alsace-Lorraine was the very symbol of victory and the emergence of Germany as the major continental power to the majority of Germans, though Bismarck had wisely opposed the annexation. Finally, most Germans considered Alsatians to be Germans, and much of the annexed portion of Lorraine was also German-speaking. Thus, French and German *amour propre* tended to work against a peaceful settlement of the Alsace-Lorraine issue. The two provinces remained a source of contention for almost a half-century after 1871, and an equitable solution to the problem did not appear to be within reach. During that time Alsace and Lorraine underwent a transformation from an intermediary zone linking the cultures of France and Germany to a barrier between the opposing sides.[2]

French opinion persistently maintained an idealized image of the plight of the lost provinces. Léon Gambetta, the prominent Third Republic politician who had taken the lead in continuing resistance against the Germans in 1870 after Napoleon III's surrender, had advised the French to "think of them always, speak of them never." It is difficult to say how much the French thought about Alsace and Lorraine, but they were reminded of them often, for many ignored Gambetta's stricture and persisted in speaking,

---

and writing, about them. The subject of the lost territories and their iden-
tification with France were favorite topics in the history curriculum of
primary schools, and young French pupils were continually reminded of
the fate of their eastern co-nationals.[3] Moreover, French novelists and
authors who had traveled in the annexed territories popularized a cherished image of the two provinces toiling under the Teutonic yoke and pin-
ing endlessly for the return of French rule. The image of the Alsatian
assiduously propagated in France was a corollary to that of the German
and no less distorted. Most observers during this period considered the
typical Alsatian to be someone who shared the essential French qualities,
though he might speak a German dialect, and who was stubbornly loyal
to *la patrie* in the face of adversity. The reality, of course, was a great deal
more complex. After an initial period of Alsatian intransigence against
annexation, in which many on both sides of the Vosges Mountains hoped
that France would reconquer the provinces in a war of revenge, hopes
faded for deliverance by French bayonets, and the pressing concerns of
everyday life more and more determined the attitudes of Alsatians and
Lorrainers toward German rule and their participation within the political
system of the German Empire.[4] It is interesting to note that throughout this
period both sides sought to use a variation of the argument of national self-
determination to legitimize its claim. While the question of who was to rule
Alsace had previously been settled by force, the emerging politics of
national identity clearly called for more nuanced methods.

The initial response of the inhabitants of Alsace and Lorraine to German
rule was overwhelmingly negative. Many opted to emigrate to France
rather than become German citizens. Those who remained yet rejected the
annexation were dubbed *protestataires*, and they voted—if they voted at
all—for Reichstag deputies who shared their rejection. However, as the
years slipped by with no sign of help from France, further resistance came
to seem futile, and there was an increasing willingness to form electoral ties
with the established German parties, particularly the Catholic Center and
the Social Democrats, in order to exert some political influence in the
Reichstag. The urge to find a political voice in everyday affairs gradually
took precedence over sentimental loyalty to France, especially as new generations came of age in the later years of the nineteenth century. Nevertheless, there was a pervasive feeling of distance, and difference, among
Alsatians vis-à-vis what were technically their fellow German citizens.

Alsace's geographical position made it a natural bridge between the
French and German cultural spheres, and it continued to serve as one to a
certain extent under German occupation. As Henri Burgelin has noted,
Alsatian intellectuals in Germany, such as René Schickele, sought to bring
greater awareness of Alsatian and French culture to the German public. At
the same time, Alsatians in France, particularly those in institutions of
higher education, including the librarian Lucien Herr at the Ecole Normale Supérieure and Henri Lichtenberger at the Sorbonne, deciphered the

enigmas of German culture for their many students.[5] Yet in spite of efforts by such prominent scholars to establish greater communication between France and Germany, popular accounts of life in the provinces, novels, and caricatures published in France continued to idolize the Alsatian and fuel hostility to German rule in Alsace. Many prominent French politicians and intellectuals who were Lorrainers by origin, such as Raymond Poincaré and Maurice Barrès, tended to be even more nationalist and intransigent toward German rule of the provinces than their Alsatian counterparts.

The territory of Alsace-Lorraine remained under German rule for almost fifty years, designated as a *Reichsland* within the newly created German Empire. As such, it did not share the federal status granted to other states in the empire. The special regime was a vexation to most of the inhabitants, who tended all the more to feel like foreigners under German rule. The eagerly anticipated constitution of 1911 stopped short of granting the Reichsland complete autonomy, which was a bitter disappointment to those, probably in the majority, who by that time were reconciled to a German rule that appeared to be permanent.[6] Large numbers of military personnel were stationed in this strategically vital border territory, and the often arrogant behavior of the soldiers aroused tensions with the inhabitants that culminated in the explosive events at Zabern in 1913. The integration of Alsace into the German economy and rail network, as well as the appointment of new officials, opened up numerous opportunities, and immigration of Germans from the rest of the Reich was considerable, with over 240,000 entering the two provinces in the years before 1914. By 1910, *Reichsdeutsche* and their descendants made up one-sixth of the population in Alsace-Lorraine, and their growing numbers were an additional cause of concern to many native inhabitants.[7]

It is important to note that, in so far as there was an Alsace-Lorraine "question," it was predominantly a French one. Germany consistently refused to recognize that there was the slightest ambiguity about the status of the annexed territory. As far as most Germans were concerned, the Treaty of Frankfurt of 1871 had settled the future status of the provinces definitively. The left-wing socialist Gustave Hervé noted that the German political parties, including the majority of German socialists, achieved a rare unity in their virtually unanimous refusal to recognize the existence of an Alsace-Lorraine question.[8] Nevertheless, the initial enthusiasm evoked among Germans by the annexation and the "return" of their Alsatian "brethren" gave way to distrust and skepticism in the face of Alsatian resistance against Germanization. There was a general distrust of Alsatians within Germany, and they were generally excluded from the German officer corps.[9] The *Westmark*, as it was sometimes termed by the more romantically inclined in Germany, proved unexpectedly reluctant to embrace its German heritage. When the prominent Pan-Germanist Heinrich Claß referred to the Alsatians as "Franco-German national hermaphrodites," he was merely expressing an extreme form of the frustration and disappointment that many Germans felt toward their "ungrateful" confrères in the recovered provinces.[10]

Remarkably few books about Alsace and Lorraine were published in Germany between 1898 and 1914. In contrast to the relative lack of concern in Germany, the topic seems to have been an obsessive one in France, where it prompted a steady stream of books and articles. One historian has suggested that French fascination with the culture of Alsace and Lorraine originated mainly from the annexation, since most Frenchmen had taken little notice of the two provinces prior to 1871.[11] Whatever the case, French authors tended to present a distorted image of life in the Reichsland, and wishful thinking on the part of the pundits sometimes obscured more ambivalent feelings among the French public toward France's erstwhile citizens beyond the Vosges. The Alsatian, in particular, represented a peculiar dilemma for French public opinion. A nostalgic vision of an Alsatian peasantry that spoke a German dialect, but nevertheless felt quite French at heart, predominated in many accounts published during this period. While the myth of the Alsatians staunchly maintaining their loyalty to France and stubbornly resisting Germanization prevailed in French views, in real life Alsatians within France faced suspicion and discrimination from many who distrusted their German-sounding names and accents and doubted their very "Frenchness." The fear that the innocent Alsatian resident in France might be a Prussian spy in disguise seems to have had a wide currency. In his memoirs of captivity in Germany during the war of 1870–1871, published at the turn of the century, Désiré Louis related that fellow prisoners from Alsace were singled out for favorable treatment by their German captors, and that in return some of them almost certainly served as informers against their fellow Frenchmen.[12] When the President of the French Senate and prominent Alsatian émigré Adolphe Scheurer-Kestner spoke out in favor of reopening the case of Alfred Dreyfus in 1897, right-wing anti-Dreyfusard critics savagely excoriated him as a "German" traitor. Dreyfus' attorney Joseph Reinach, also of Alsatian origin, received even harsher treatment from self-proclaimed French patriots. While many French observers noted with pride the large numbers of Alsatians who enlisted in the Foreign Legion, only a handful recorded the prejudice and hostility that such recruits often faced from their officers.[13] Few of those writing about Alsace were openly willing to recognize the hypocrisy of French opinion regarding Alsatians.

One substantial minority group in Alsace was almost entirely left out of the sentimental musings on the lost provinces by French authors. The Jews of Alsace, though they formed more than half of the Jewish population of France before 1871, were conspicuous by their absence from popular novels and travelogues about Alsace before 1914. Alsatian Jews remained overwhelmingly loyal to France and frequently chose to face the hardships of emigration in order to remain French citizens. Many of those who did not choose to leave the province were strong supporters of the *protestataire* movement in the province before the turn of the century. As was the case with their Christian counterparts, relations between German and Alsatian Jews were very strained.[14] Clearly both groups were sufficiently assimilated to their respective nations by 1871 that national loyalties overrode religious ties. Lucien Aaron, who wrote using the pseudonym Georges Delahache, one of the few Alsatian Jews to publish a major book on the Alsace-Lorraine question during the years under examination, was a staunch revanchard, as was the most famous Jew of Alsatian origin, Alfred Dreyfus.[15] However, in spite of the reservoir of affection that Alsatian Jews demonstrated toward France, they were virtually nonexistent in popular accounts of Alsace during the period. If one had only these books and pamphlets as evidence, one could easily imagine that there were no Jews in Alsace at all. Clearly Jews held a precarious position in the relatively recent self-image constructed by the French.

The Dreyfus Affair and the ferocious anti-Semitism accompanying it came as a rude shock to Alsatian Jews. Dreyfus was usually attacked in anti-Semitic caricature both as a Jew and as an Alsatian, speaking French with a German or Yiddish accent. As the historian Vicki Caron has demonstrated, the loyalty of Alsatian Jews toward France was profoundly shaken by this display of race hatred. The result was the emergence of a greater willingness of those Alsatian Jews who remained in the province to work within the framework of the German Empire.[16] Similarly, Alsatian Catholics were alarmed by the anticlerical legislation enacted in the French republic after 1903, and their consequent disillusionment with France made cooperation with Germany seem more palatable now that the *Kulturkampf* was a thing of the past. Thus, two groups that had maintained a strong loyalty toward France were drifting toward *de facto* understandings with the German authorities in the years following the turn of the century, at least partly as a result of events within France.

The myth of the loyal Alsatians and Lorrainers patiently suffering under German rule as they awaited deliverance by France nevertheless remained a powerful and persistent image in French representations of the lost provinces before 1914. The writer Alphonse Daudet made an early, and lasting, contribution to the myth of the heroic Alsatian. His popular short story "La dernière classe," first published in the collection *Contes du lundi* in 1873, had as its subject the final lesson of a small-town French teacher in Alsace, M. Hamel, as seen through the eyes of Franz (naturally), one of his young charges. The "Prussians" have decreed that German will henceforth be the language of instruction, and M. Hamel accordingly is due to resign from his position the following day. Franz, unaware of the impending change, notes with surprise on arriving at school that Hamel is dressed in his best Sunday clothes, and that a number of the adult villagers are also in attendance. When M. Hamel informs the class of the order from Berlin, Franz is devastated, and suddenly regrets his strict teacher's departure and the impending loss of the French texts he has heretofore found so tedious and heavy. M. Hamel expresses his sorrow that the Alsatians have not learned the French language more assiduously, and that he himself was not more demanding of his pupils. Finally, the lesson over, M. Hamel is overcome with emotion, and as the trumpets of the drilling German troops sound through the windows, he writes "Vive la France" on the blackboard and dismisses his pupils for the last time. A similar episode occurs in a popular French song of the era, "Le maître d'école alsacien," in which the Alsatian schoolmaster exhorts his students to have courage in the face of Alsace's separation from France:

Enfants, vous qu'a frappés la guerre,	Children, you whom the war has struck,
Souvenez-vous de nos malheurs,	Remember our misfortunes,
Et que la nouvelle frontière	And that the new frontier
N'existe jamais pour vos coeurs.	Never exists in your hearts.
Les yeux tournés vers la patrie,	Keep your eyes turned toward *la patrie*
Grandissez; l'heure sonnera,	As you grow up; the hour will sound,
Où son âme aujourd'hui meurtrie	When its soul, today so battered,
Vers elle vous rappellera.	Will call you toward it.[17]

In a book devoted to the lost provinces, the native Lorrainer Maurice Barrès evoked the plight of similar former teachers of French in Alsace and Lorraine, many of them now indigent from the loss of their livelihood.[18] The image of the expelled French instructor clearly struck a popular chord as a symbol of French displacement from Alsace-Lorraine and the heavy-handed German cultural oppression that followed.

French writers also broached the subject of German incursion at a more intimate level in the conquered provinces. In *L'oubli?* their novel of 1899, Théodore Cahu and Louis Forest portray the travails of the Stockmanns, a German-speaking family of Metz. A German lieutenant, Fritz von Schnabelkraft, falls in love with the young Louise Stockmann. When he rescues her after she falls through the ice in a skating accident, Louise's father is far from grateful toward this "Ostrogoth" for rescuing his daughter. Michel Stockmann is a *protestataire*, stubbornly resistant toward the Prussian overlords. Fritz gradually undergoes a change of heart in his narrow worship of things German, thanks to his infatuation with Louise and his reading of Heinrich Heine's writings on France.[19] Nevertheless, after Fritz asks permission to marry Louise, Michel Stockmann flies into a rage, brutally beating his daughter, whom he derisively refers to as *la Prussienne*. Louise flees to Baden with Fritz. Although she is welcomed by Fritz's family, she feels stifled in Germany, where the women are heavy and inelegant and the men unbearably pedantic. Louise increasingly becomes convinced that there is an unbridgeable chasm between the two countries. Michel Stockmann meanwhile becomes disillusioned with his faith in France as the years roll by with no sign of redemption from Teutonic rule. Peter Schilling, a young exile whom Stockmann and the local curé had persuaded to leave Alsace and enroll in the Foreign Legion many years before, returns embittered by the hostility and hardship he has experienced in France and berates the two old men for advising him to leave home. By the novel's end, everyone is disillusioned with earlier hopes, whether for a war of revanche or for a peaceful solution of the Alsace-Lorraine question by both countries, and the German occupation continues with no end in sight.

A motif that recurred frequently in popular literary depictions of Alsace in France during this period was the escape across the frontier, preferably enlivened by an account of German border guards firing their rifles in hot pursuit. This image, a precursor of the imagery associated with the Iron Curtain, was first established in the popular imagination by the enormously popular children's book *Le tour de la France par deux enfants*, originally published in 1877 and appearing in dozens of editions thereafter.[20] The book recounts the adventures of two young Alsatian brothers, André and Julien Volden, following the death of their father during the hostilities of 1870–1871. The two boys decide to leave their home town of Phalsbourg and risk a surreptitious crossing of the frontier, so that they might fulfill their dying father's wish that they grow up as Frenchmen. They succeed with the aid of many well-wishers, and thus begin their memorable wanderings through the beloved land of France and their investigation of the French spirit. The two brothers are never in doubt about their French identity, nor are those whom they encounter during their travels.

The best-known border flight occurs in René Bazin's famous novel *Les Oberlé*. The Oberlé family consists of three generations who, in their varying reactions to the plight of Alsace, represent the hard choices faced by many Alsatians. Nevertheless, it is not difficult to see where Bazin's sympathies lie. Jean Oberlé, a young Alsatian of middle-class origin, returns from a course of study in Germany, where he has learned to admire certain German qualities, but has also discovered the Frenchman in himself. He is supported by his grandfather, Philippe Oberlé, and his uncle, Ulrich Bieler, old men in whom faith in France lives on. However, he faces the opposition of his ambitious father Joseph, who had trained for a career in the French administration, but went over to the Germans after the annexation. Joseph's wife, Monique, who despises the Germans but quietly suffers through many social occasions with German officials in order to further her husband's ambitions, supports her son's stand. Lucienne, Jean's sister, who has attended a German lycée and acquired an enthusiasm for German culture, supports her father in his ambitions. Joseph manages the family's lumber mill, where he has hired numerous German employees, who are more willing than the locals to submit to his autocratic style. Bazin portrays the German workers as a sullen crew, cut off from contact with the surrounding population, with whom they share no bond of kinship, origin, religion, or custom. They fear authority without respecting it, and desire to wreak vengeance for their miserable lot on the Alsatians when the Germans become more numerous.[21] They offer a stark contrast to the simple, kindly people of Alsace whom Jean encounters during his forays through the mountains. German officials for their part show no such restraint in making known their plans of aggression. Wilhelm von Farnow, a school friend of Jean who is now an officer stationed in Alsace, explains to Jean that the Germans are born for the conquest of the world, and that conquerors are neither soft nor just.[22] Lucienne's revelation that she is engaged to be married to Farnow comes as a rude shock to Jean, and is the last of a series of events that drives him to flee to France. Jean determines to cross the frontier, and succeeds, though he is slightly wounded in a hail of gunfire from the border guards. We are left to ponder his ultimate fate, but clearly we are led to believe that France will welcome the young hero with open arms.

The older generations of Alsatians, those with a memory of French rule, were widely believed in France to be mainstays of resistance to "Prussianization." In his poem "Papa Tricolore," Théodore Botrel presents an idealized grandfather figure, a veteran of the Napoleonic wars.[23] The evocation of Napoleonic victories over Prussia stands in stark contrast to the defeats of the second emperor. These come as a shock to the old Alsatian, who, "going to bed French, awoke as a Prussian!" Eventually, the old man is arrested and taken to Strasbourg, where German authorities accuse him of talking of revanche and wearing the tricolor badge, as well as inciting schoolchildren to acts of disobedience with mocking comments about the Germans. Condemned to prison, he dies broken-hearted, a martyr to Alsace and the memory of "the little corporal." Many authors likewise idealized the younger generation in Alsace, imagining it to be imbued with a devotion to France though it did not share its parents' memories of French rule. In his novel *Juste Lobel, Alsacien*, André Lichtenberger describes the decision of his hero, the secretary general of a pacifist organization, to return to his Alsatian homeland after many years' absence. Juste is reunited with his beloved nurse, Salomé, and her son Jean Knabel. The latter is a very Teutonic-looking young man, but nevertheless faces frequent abuse during his mandatory service in the German army because he is Alsatian.[24] Subsequently, Juste is shocked to witness the arrest of Jean for desertion.[25] This and other acts of German brutality in Alsace come as severe blows to his deluded hopes for a peaceful understanding between France and Germany, and he is thus forced to re-evaluate his commitment to international pacifism. Juste comes to the realization that he has embraced the movement partly out of infatuation with Hilda Sverdrup, a prominent Swedish pacifist, feminist, and vegetarian. However, Juste's confession of affection leaves Hilda unmoved. Juste now recognizes her as an asexual being, an unnatural androgyne, just as pacifism stands revealed to him as a rootless cosmopolitanism lacking in virility. The patriotic awakening Juste experiences restores him to a healthy frame of mind, and he rejects his pacifist inclinations so that he may identify himself fully with the French nation.

French travelogues about Alsace and Lorraine published during these years were uniformly hostile to German rule. Most were by Alsatian émigrés, who tended to confect sentimental visions of the days of French rule. Books by Georges Delahache, Georges Ducrocq, André Hallays, Emile Hinzelin, and Gaston Phélip seemed designed to meet an anticipated demand by the French public for portrayals of hearty resistance to pig-headed German authority in the provinces. The tone bordered on the religious in many cases, with hagiographic depictions of heroes and lesser-known mortals of the Alsatian pantheon in the struggle against Teutonic darkness. In his book *Coeurs d'Alsace et de Lorraine*, Emile Hinzelin describes a "pilgrimage" of six young students organized by a certain Professor Justin Lucrot to the Reichsland.[26] Each of the students follows a separate itinerary, and collects edifying tales of heroism on the part of the local inhabitants, as well as anecdotes about the gauche Germans. In *Voix d'Alsace et de Lorraine*, Gaston Phélip provides portraits of prominent political figures in the two provinces, and leaves no doubt where his sympathies lie.[27] Phélip's heroes include M. Samain, the young president of the Jeunesse Lorraine and an avid nationalist, and the Abbé Wetterlé, a prominent *protestataire* and deputy to the Reichstag from Colmar. By contrast, anyone who works within the German system, however innocuously, particularly Reichstag deputies and pro-German newspaper owners, receives the full ire of Phélip's pen. Such black-and-white versions of the Alsace-Lorraine question tended to discourage constructive dialogue.

The travel accounts and descriptions of Alsace-Lorraine published in France during these years did more to confirm than to refute literary stereotypes. A favorite subject of many French observers writing about their travels in Alsace and Lorraine was the desecration of towns and cities in the provinces with examples of the bombastic architecture favored in German official buildings of the period. It was unfortunate for German rule in the provinces that it did indeed coincide with an era of rampant bad taste in architecture, not confined to Germany. In his travel memoir, André Hallays noted that the ugliness of German public buildings in Alsace was amplified by their colossal size.[28] Georges Ducrocq likewise thought that a typical visitor to the center of Metz would assume it was a Germanized city and quickly become bored.[29] The arch Germanophobe Jeanne Régamey described the graceless German architecture of Strasbourg as bearing the mark of the Prussian boot, "defaced by its brutal heel that reduces all spirit, all idealism, and all enthusiasm to utter mediocrity."[30] Emile Hinzelin also provided an extensive cataloguing of examples of architectural crimes committed by the Germans in Alsace.[31] One Russian observer sympathetic to the French noted that it was probably unwise to place a statue of Wilhelm I in Strasbourg, where it served constantly to remind the inhabitants of their subjection.[32] The point of these authors was that Germany was attempting to stamp its character on the conquered provinces with its building projects, but the results only set them off more fully from the local population. Alsace and Lorraine proved to be the front line in a clash of taste that the Germans, during this period at least, were ill-equipped to win.

One of the best-known writers from the conquered provinces, indeed one of the most prominent literary figures of his generation, was the Lorrainer Maurice Barrès. Barrès was a fiery French ultra-patriot much admired even by his enemies and commanded a great deal of influence among young French intellectuals. In addition to producing numerous novels and essays, he was a major contributor to a nationalist review devoted to the conquered provinces, *Les Marches de l'Est*, which appeared in 1909 and ran until the outbreak of the war. Barrès also served as a right-wing deputy in the National Assembly. The image of the Germans propagated by Barrès was extremely crude, bordering on caricature, and he played a disproportionate role in disseminating a distorted view of Germans.

In his novels about the "eastern marches," as elsewhere in his massive oeuvre, Barrès developed his theory of an intimate link between culture and soil. Barrès abhorred what he saw as the modern tendency to uproot people from their ancestral environment by way of industrialization and urbanization in the name of "progress." The development of modern society, according to Barrès, threatened to undermine the synergy established through the centuries between the people of rural France and their immediate surroundings, the connection between soil and blood being at least as potent as that between parents and children. It was precisely this feeling of kinship with the *patrie* that made the German occupation of Alsace and Lorraine particularly galling to Barrès. The German interlopers in the Lorraine of Barrès's imagination are accordingly drawn in the sharpest possible contrast to the native French inhabitants. For Barrès, the French represented the highest attainment of individual responsibility and free will, while the Germans were enslaved by imaginary laws of universal determinism. Hence, any attempt to bring the two cultures together in the same space must inevitably fail, like trying to mix oil and water. While effective in its simplicity, Barrès's conception of German character was so crude that it ultimately strained credulity and hindered his argument.

In Barrès's novels about Lorraine, the proximity of the occupiers to the sacred soil of France only served to accentuate further the barbarism of the Germans. In *Au service de l'Allemagne* (1905), Barrès describes the impressions of Paul Ehrmann, a young Lorrainer and medical student who has served in the German army. Ehrmann's experiences have made him increasingly aware of the basic incompatibility of French and German national characters. Stationed in Alsace, Ehrmann observes German officers in Strasbourg conducting themselves like foreign conquerors, but a fight he witnesses between Alsatians and Germans in a *café concert* ends with the oppressed Alsatians emerging triumphant.[33] Ehrmann's service in the German army only confirms his initial negative impressions of the Germans. The common soldiers are completely lacking in spirit and individual initiative, and the officers are invariably brutal toward the lower ranks. Barrès thought he perceived a close link between the German spirit and Protestantism, which he saw as a religion that preached "devotion to work, the feeling of responsibility before God and men, a horror of sins of the flesh: it lets slumber the spirit of generosity, of sacrifice, and of heroism."[34] Ehrmann accordingly observes that the essential virtues of the French—urbanity, generosity, and altruism—are completely lacking among the Germans he encounters.[35]

Barrès took the contrast between French and German a step further in *Colette Baudoche* (1909). The main German character of the novel is Frédéric Asmus, a young professor from Koenigsberg who lodges with the Baudoche family of Metz. Asmus is well-meaning, though ponderous and lacking in quick wit, and devotes himself to a careful study of French culture. However, he is unable to grasp the nuances of being French, because he does not share the intimate connection with his surroundings felt by the native inhabitants. He is also crude and thoughtless in his habits, and thoroughly pedantic—in the Barrèsian universe, grace and charm are clearly acquired from nature rather than nurture.[36] Ultimately, Asmus comes to appreciate the charm of the French city, in a limited way, with the help of his host family, and he becomes enamored of the daughter Colette. However, he realizes that an unbridgeable chasm lies between him and Colette, reflecting that between the two peoples, and that no amount of good will can suffice for crossing either.

The cherished image of the lost provinces awaiting rescue by their French sister provinces found its visual counterpart in a revealing artistic motif. Caricaturists frequently portrayed Alsace as a young woman, in distinctive Alsatian dress, detained against her will. She was usually closely watched by her captors, at times even blindfolded and held by force. Such images were intended to bring a host of associations to mind. The clearly unchivalrous attitudes toward the fair sex echoed the atrocity stories that had circulated during and after the war of 1870–1871, in which German soldiers usually figured as savage brutes, particularly in their treatment of women. The image of a woman detained also suggested a highly visible monument to the fate of Alsace and Lorraine in the heart of Paris. In the Place de la Concorde, where sculptural allegories of the major French cities were on display, the statue representing Strasbourg had been covered with shrouds ever since the surrender of the provinces, as an abiding visual metaphor for French defeat and loss. Nor was the hint of rape lost on contemporaries. The image of Alsace as female hostage thus played on crude mythologies of a "German" code of conduct that contrasted markedly with that the French had of themselves (figs. 6 and 7).

One of the most popular and successful of all French caricaturists during this period was the Alsatian Hansi (the pen name of Jean-Jacques Waltz). Like Barrès, Hansi created images of the Germans that were hostile and sometimes crude, but unlike the novelist he had a light touch and

FIGURE 6: Alsace as woman held hostage I
(Emile Hinzelin, *L'Alsace sous le joug*. Paris: Editions et Librairie, 1914)

his drawings were almost always amusing. His love of Alsace and the regret he felt at its separation from France permeate his work of the period. Hansi's *Histoire d'Alsace* is a delightful illustrated romp through the history of the provinces, written for children, in which barbaric Germans through the ages, invariably wearing spectacles and displaying a penchant for stealing clocks, cast covetous eyes across the Rhine toward the fortunate land of their Alsatian brethren. Hansi's colorful drawings

Figure 7: Alsace as woman held hostage II
(Gaston Phélip, *Voix d'Alsace et de Lorraine*. Paris: Editions et Librairie, 1911)

and keen wit, as well as his sentimental portrayals of Alsatian life, won him a large following in France, and his works circulated widely.[37]

In spite of the strong sentiments associated with the subject of Alsace-Lorraine on both sides of the frontier, there were voices calling for a peaceful reconciliation of Franco-German disputes over the status of the two provinces. The journalist John Grand-Carteret correctly observed that, although the cult of Alsace flourished in France, the French public would not commit itself to a war of revanche merely to reconquer the lost provinces; he therefore considered a peaceful settlement inevitable.[38] The Alsatian writer Jean Heimweh recognized the impossibility of a lasting peace in Europe based on the status quo, and in addition considered a Franco-German rapprochement a necessity in the face of the growing menace of Anglo-American power.[39] Heimweh was willing to recognize the importance of the Reichsland to Germany, both as a defensive glacis against France and as a symbol of German unity.[40] His compromise solution was autonomy for the two provinces within the German Empire. The pacifist Adolphe Aderer hoped for Franco-German reconciliation through a negotiated settlement of the Alsace-Lorraine question, with a possible cession of the French-speaking territory to France in return for colonial concessions.[41] Marcel Laurent and Albert Gobat, both concerned by the specter of European war and the enormous costs of the arms race, argued that a peaceful settlement of the Alsace-Lorraine question was a central necessity to guarantee the peace of the continent.[42] The socialist Gustave Hervé considered it possible to arrange an exchange of the two provinces in return for massive economic concessions to Germany from France.[43] The German writer Otto Flake, a "new Alsatian" (*Neuelsäßer*) born of German immigrants to Alsace, published one of the most intelligent and thoughtful books on the Alsatian question in Germany during these years. Flake stressed the cultural gulf between most Germans and Alsatians caused by the location of Alsace in the French orbit for over two centuries. Alsatians had greater egalitarianism, as well as more warmth in social relations, particularly as compared with North Germans.[44] Flake believed that the German system of government, a collection of contradictions, was in sharp contrast to the centralized government of France. Hence, autonomy was a natural solution, acceptable to both countries, of the problem of Alsace. In spite of all such suggestions, a compromise satisfactory to both sides proved elusive. France and Germany assigned too much symbolic importance to the provinces for either side to consider making concessions, and in the end the issue was settled only by armed conflict instead.

Zabern

The Zabern Affair dramatically demonstrated the limits of Alsatian integration into the German Empire. The affair itself grew from ludicrously petty beginnings. Zabern, a garrison town in northern Alsace, was widely believed to be the "most German" Alsatian town. Nevertheless, the town had its share of the tensions present throughout Alsace between local inhabitants and Reich Germans. The affair began when a young lieutenant, Baron Günter von Forstner, used the pejorative term *Wackes* to refer to Alsatians, within earshot of local recruits. As word of Forstner's utterances spread through the town, resentment increased, and Forstner faced hostile crowds on the street and outside his residence, necessitating an armed escort. There were ugly scenes between soldiers and civilians, culminating in a series of street clashes in which dozens of civilians, mainly young men, were arrested. It was clear to many even in Germany that the German army had overstepped the bounds first of propriety, then of legality. The affair caused a great deal of unrest in Alsace and even threatened to touch off a major constitutional debate in the Reichstag over civilian oversight of the German military.[45]

Coverage of Zabern by the French press varied in tone, and there was disagreement about the meaning and ultimate significance of the events. However, there was general amusement at the embarrassment caused to the German military and the incompetent response of German officers. The final days of the affair, when young men were being arrested in the streets of the town for laughing at passing soldiers, saw a mixture of mirth and outrage in the French newspapers. A typical headline in *Le Matin* read: "Under the Prussian Heel: The Role of Terror in Saverne: A Child Talks and Is Arrested; A Passerby Laughs and Is Arrested."[46] The events at Zabern seemed to confirm deep-rooted French stereotypes of the lack of humor and finesse among brutal German officials, and called forth in the French press many expressions of sympathy for the unfortunate Alsatians. Even in the German press there was a predominant opinion that, while probably beginning with a misunderstanding, the affair was compounded by the clumsiness of the authorities. However, though the affair quickly raised passions on both sides, it was just as quickly forgotten with the coming of war the following summer.

Conclusion

The mythical Alsatians portrayed by their putative friends and allies effectively obscured the plight of the real Alsatians. Few French and Germans could really empathize with the real-life dilemmas faced by the inhabitants of the Reichsland. It was far easier to accept the cherished images and urge drastic solutions from a distance than to encourage intricate compromises. The respective French and German mythologies of the suffering patriots and the returning brethren tended to discourage openings to the other side of the divide, and there was no official Franco-German discussion on the fate of the conquered provinces. The inversion of values occurred at two levels on both sides. Both French and Germans tended to project an idealized portrait of the Alsatian while harboring distrust for the actual inhabitants of the lost/regained province. At the same time, both considered their control of the province to be the ideal state of affairs, without much regard for the feelings of the Alsatians themselves.

In his well-known work on the response of public opinion in France to the outbreak of World War I, Jean-Jacques Becker noted that Alsace and

Lorraine held little place in the minds of most French citizens during the early days of August 1914. While an interest in Alsace-Lorraine was a central point in the nationalist revival among educated French youth during the prewar years, this enthusiasm did not extend to the general population.[47] In spite of all the sentimental evocations of past links and the undoubted sympathy for the plight of France's former subjects, there was little enthusiasm among the general public for a war of reconquest.[48] Nevertheless, shortly before the outbreak of hostilities, prime minister René Viviani declared that though France would take up arms unwillingly in the face of German aggression, it would not put them down again until Alsace-Lorraine had been regained. During the previous years, the lost provinces had held the imagination of the French General Staff. Plan XVII, the outline for offensive operations in the event of war, called for a large-scale advance directly into Alsace. It appears that, in this case at least, the desire for revanche overcame strategic judgement. Well-prepared German troops, fully expecting an attack, inflicted thousands of casualties on the advancing French, and the latter were forced to retreat. Alsace and Lorraine had to wait four more years for their "liberation."

Notes

1. Georges Ducrocq, *La blessure mal fermée: notes d'un voyageur en Alsace-Lorraine* (Paris: Plon-Nourrit, 1910).
2. See, for example, Maxime Leroy, *L'Alsace-Lorraine: porte de France, porte d'Allemagne …* (Paris: P. Ollendorff, 1914).
3. See Mona Ozouf, "L'Alsace-Lorraine, mode d'emploi. La question d'Alsace-Lorraine dans le *Manuel général*, 1871–1914," *L'école de la France: essais sur la Révolution, l'utopie, et l'enseignement* (Paris: Editions Gallimard, 1984), pp. 214–230. Nevertheless, Ozouf notes that there was a gradual falling off of mentions of Alsace-Lorraine in the *Manuel général* by the turn of the century.
4. The best general work on Alsace-Lorraine under German rule is Dan P. Silverman, *Reluctant Union: Alsace-Lorraine and Imperial Germany 1871–1918* (University Park: The Pennsylvania State University Press, 1972).
5. Henri Burgelin, "Le mythe de l'ennemi héréditaire dans les relations franco-allemandes," *Documents: Revue des questions allemandes* (1979): 85.
6. See Jean Marie Mayeur, *Autonomie et politique en Alsace: la constitution de 1911* (Paris: A. Colin, 1970). Two contemporary and predictably critical accounts written by Frenchmen of the constitutional development of Alsace-Lorraine within the German Empire are Robert Baldy, *L'Alsace-Lorraine et l'empire allemand (1871–1911)* (Paris, Nancy: Berger-Levrault, 1912) and Philippe Gerber, *La condition de l'Alsace-Lorraine dans l'Empire Allemand* (Lille: H. Morel, 1906).
7. Christian Baechler, "Das Verhalten der Elsaß-Lothringer im Deutschen Reich (1871–1918)," in Franz Knipping and Ernst Weisenfeld, eds., *Eine ungewöhnliche Geschichte: Deutschland, Frankreich seit 1870* (Bonn: Europa Union Verlag, 1988), p. 51.
8. Gustave Hervé, *L'Alsace-Lorraine* (Paris: Editions de "La Guerre Sociale," 1913), pp. 46–47. A German edition of Hervé's book appeared the same year.

9. Hans-Ulrich Wehler, "Unfähig zur Verfassungsreform: Das Reichsland Elsaß-Lothringen von 1870 bis 1918," in *Krisenherde des Kaiserreichs* (Göttingen: Vandenhoeck and Ruprecht, 1970), p. 47.

10. Heinrich Claß, *Wenn ich der Kaiser wär': Politische Wahrheiten und Notwendigkeiten* (Leipzig: Dieterich, 1913), p. 84.

11. Frederic H. Seager, "The Alsace-Lorraine Question in France, 1871–1914," in Charles K. Warner, ed., *From the Ancien Regime to the Popular Front* (New York: Columbia University Press, 1969), p. 112.

12. Désiré Louis, *Souvenirs d'un prisonnier de guerre en Allemagne (1870–1871)* (Paris: F. Juven, 1899), pp. 81–82, 88–90.

13. See, for example, Emile Hinzelin, *L'Alsace sous le joug* (Paris: Editions et librairie, 1914), pp. 23–28.

14. Vicki Caron, *Between France and Germany: The Jews of Alsace-Lorraine, 1871–1918* (Stanford: Stanford University Press, 1988), pp. 109–110.

15. Georges Delahache, *Alsace-Lorraine: la carte au liséré vert*, 4th ed. (Paris: Hachette, 1911).

16. Caron, *Between France and Germany*, pp. 128–133.

17. Madeleine Schmidt, ed., *Chansons de la revanche et de la grande guerre* (Nancy: Presse universitaires de Nancy, 1985), p. 49.

18. Maurice Barrès, *Alsace-Lorraine* (Paris: E. Sansot, 1906), p. 11.

19. Théodore Cahu and Louis Forest, *L'oubli?* (Published as a supplement to *L'Illustration*, 29 July 1899–4 November 1899): 52.

20. G. Bruno, *Le tour de la France par deux enfants* (Paris: Librairie Classique Eugène Belin, 1877), pp. 18–25. G. Bruno was the pen name of the wife of the sociologist Alfred Fouillée, whose work on national character I have referred to previously.

21. René Bazin, *Les Oberlé* (Paris: Calmann-Lévy, 1901), pp. 126–127.

22. Ibid., p. 217.

23. Théodore Botrel, *Coups de clairon: chants et poèmes héroïques* (Paris: G. Ondet, 1903), pp. 101–105.

24. André Lichtenberger, *Juste Lobel, Alsacien* (Paris: Plon, 1911), pp. 129–130.

25. Ibid., pp. 232–235.

26. 3rd. ed. Paris: Librairie Delagrave, 1913.

27. Paris: Editions et Librairie, 1911.

28. André Hallays, *A travers l'Alsace* (Paris: Perrin et Cie., 1911), pp. 90–91.

29. Ducrocq, *La blessure mal fermée*, p. 8.

30. Jeanne Régamey, *Jeune Alsace: roman* (Paris: Nouvelle librairie nationale, 1909), p. 74.

31. Hinzelin, *L'Alsace sous le joug*, pp. 72–81.

32. J. Novicow, *L'Alsace-Lorraine: obstacle à l'expansion allemande* (Paris: Felix Alcan, 1913), pp. 154–155.

33. *L'œuvre de Maurice Barrès*, vol. 6 (Paris: Club de l'Honnête Homme, 1966), pp. 45–48.

34. Ibid., p. 107.

35. Ibid., p. 113.

36. Ibid., pp. 180–181.

37. Hansi, *L'Histoire d'Alsace: racontée aux petits enfants d'Alsace et de France* (Paris: H. Floury, 1913). For Hansi's biography, see Jorg von Uthmann, *Le diable est-il allemand?: 200 ans de préjugés franco-allemands* (Paris: Denoel, 1984), pp. 137–138. Hansi was arrested by German authorities and condemned to one year in prison shortly before the war, but succeeded in escaping to France. See Thomas Raithel, *Das "Wunder" der inneren Einheit: Studien zur deutschen und französischen Öffentlichkeit bei Beginn des Ersten Weltkrieges* (Bonn: Bouvier Verlag, 1996), pp. 110–111. The Nazis remembered Hansi's influence, and his works were accordingly banned in Alsace during the second German occupation.

38. John Grand-Carteret, *Le rapprochement franco-allemand par l'amélioration du sort de l'Alsace-Lorraine* (Bonn: A. Ahn, 1911), p. 4.

39. Jean Heimweh [pseud. of Fernand de Dartein], *Allemagne, France, Alsace-Lorraine* (Paris: Armand Colin, 1899), pp. 5–8.

40. Ibid., pp. 13–15.
41. Adolphe Aderer, *Vers la fin d'une haine* (Paris: Calmann-Lévy, 1907), pp. 25–30.
42. Marcel Laurent, *La paix armée et le problème d'Alsace dans l'opinion des nouvelles générations françaises* (Paris: n.p., 1914) and Albert Gobat, *Le cauchemar de l'Europe* (Strasbourg and Paris: Treuttel and Wurtz; Le Soudier, 1911).
43. Gustave Hervé, *L'Alsace-Lorraine*, p. 137.
44. Otto Flake, *Rund um die elsässische Frage* (Karlsruhe: Dreililien Verlag, 1911), pp. 49–50.
45. The best account of the affair is David Schoenbaum, *Zabern 1913: Consensus Politics in Imperial Germany* (London: George Allen and Unwin, 1982); see also Hans-Ulrich Wehler, "Symbol des halbabsolutistischen Herrschaftssystems: Der Fall Zabern von 1913/14 als Verfassungskrise des Wilhelminischen Kaiserreichs," in *Krisenherde des Kaiserreichs*, pp. 65–83. For a full contemporary account, see Hinzelin, *L'Alsace sous le joug*, pp. 1–11.
46. *Le Matin*, 1 December 1913.
47. Agathon [pseud. of Alexis de Tarde and Henri Massis], *Les jeunes gens d'aujourd'hui* (Paris: Plon-Nourrit, 1913), pp. 38–40.
48. Jean-Jacques Becker, *1914: Comment les français sont entrés dans la guerre* (Paris: Presses de la Fondation nationale des sciences politiques, 1977), p. 62. See also the evaluation of 5 February 1914 by the German ambassador in Paris, von Schoen which discounts French desire for war over Alsace-Lorraine, in *Die große Politik der Europäischen Kabinette, 1871–1914: Sammlung der diplomatischen Akten des Auswärtigen Amtes*, ed. by Johannes Lepsius, Albrecht Mendelssohn-Bartholdy, and Friedrich Thimme (Berlin: Deutsche Verlagsgesellschaft für Politik und Geschichte, 1922–1927), vol. 39, pp. 248–250.

Chapter Five

SHADES OF OPINION:
THE POLITICAL SPECTRUM

> It [the German people] thinks only of the dangers, real or imaginary, that
> threaten it. Domestic enemies no longer suffice for its vigilance, it seeks
> others outside; the feeling of insecurity is growing. Confidence in the
> government is not the only thing that is slipping away; the nation is even
> losing confidence in itself. A veritable militarist frenzy has seized it, and
> armaments bill succeeds armaments bill, while the power of the country
> never seems sufficiently protected.
>
> William Martin, *La crise politique de l'Allemagne contemporaine*[1]

Modern politics is the realm of symbolism *par excellence*, and France and
Germany in the years before World War I were no exceptions to this rule.
In the realm of mass electoral politics, parties found themselves forced to
resort to symbolic manipulation in order to get their message across to the
electorate. Foreign policy was not usually a high priority for parliamentary politicians, except in times of crisis that were not conducive to reflection and carefully considered decision-making. Unfortunately, much of
the period under examination was dominated by a succession of just such
crises in international politics, many of them rising from long-term conditions that were beyond the ken of the general public. Political figures in
both countries tended to share the preconceptions and prejudices of their
constituencies, and the political process tended to reinforce a simplified
view of what the military and foreign policy establishment of the other
country was up to. The image of the enemy was hardly uniform throughout the population in either France or Germany. There were differences
based on educational level, social class, and, not least, political identifica-
tion. Nevertheless, there was a greater consistency across the political
spectrum than one might expect. The distorted image of the opposite
nation even took root on the political left and among pacifists, both groups
devoted to certain theories of international reconciliation and solidarity.

Notes for this chapter begin on page 104.

The Left

The failure of French and German socialists to act according to their internationalist principles and mobilize against the outbreak of war in 1914 must be considered one of the tragic missed opportunities of the twentieth century. In the elections of 1912, the German Social Democratic Party, or SPD, achieved its greatest victory since its foundation, becoming the largest faction in the Reichstag. At the same time, the French Socialists, split since their foundation, were becoming a unified party with a common program and a growing appeal to French workers. French and German socialists had protested against the threat of war in their respective countries during the crisis provoked by the Balkan Wars in 1912–1913. However, when war did come, socialists in both countries supported their governments and entered the fray, willingly in France and enthusiastically in Germany. In the first half of 1914, the Second International was arguably at the height of its influence in Europe. Five years and millions of dead later, the unity of European socialism, already shattered by war, was further fragmented by the great schism between socialists and communists just as it began to face unprecedented challenges in the form of fascist and authoritarian regimes.

It was a well-known tenet of the Second International that the working class of a given country had more in common with workers of other countries than with the bourgeoisie of its own. It was also an article of socialist doctrine that war was an inevitable product of the capitalist world order; some even went so far as to argue (with Lenin) that war was a necessary prerequisite for the destruction of that order in a world revolution. The bourgeoisie used patriotic rhetoric to rally the working classes for imperialist war in the name of "national interest"—so the argument ran—but national solidarity was quickly forgotten when the aims of the ruling classes had been achieved. The real enemy, accordingly, was capitalism, and the agents of capitalism who were closest at hand were those in the workers' own countries. Thus, the French and German working classes could not possibly have any interest in the imperial rivalries of their respective governments, as the benefits of modern war accrued solely to the ruling classes. However, as was so often the case in the international socialist movement, the distance between theory and practice made for a much more complicated picture.

The major obstacle facing a realistic appraisal of Franco-German relations by French and German socialists was that socialist theorists in both countries generally tended to take an excessively abstract approach to the problem of war and militarism in international affairs. When it came to specific instances of heightened tensions between France and Germany, socialists had to resort to *ad hoc* measures to deal with the crises. Although there was frequent discussion in the International of the option of a general strike and refusal to mobilize by the workers in the event of a major

European war, there was little precise planning for such a contingency. Worse still, there was neither a long-term design to improve Franco-German relations nor, given the rules in both the French and German socialist parties against participation in bourgeois governments, the wherewithal to put one into operation. The situation was further complicated by rifts in the socialist leadership in both countries. Briefly stated, the major split was between orthodox Marxists, who continued to argue the desirability of revolution and class war, and revisionists (or reformists), who believed that a peaceful transition to socialism was possible through electoral success and parliamentary participation. At least until the outbreak of war in 1914, revisionists were likely to favor working with the bourgeois parties and even share many of their preconceptions regarding foreign policy. In both France and Germany before 1914, much of the rhetoric continued to be revolutionary and internationalist, but the trend among socialist parties, backed by the more moderate trade unions, was toward reform and engagement in national politics. The relatively abstract notion of international solidarity of the workers could easily give way in the course of parliamentary maneuvering to more material concerns, such as wages and working conditions.[2]

Finally, and perhaps most importantly, the rank and file of the French and German socialist parties did not live in a world sealed off from nonsocialist influences. In both France and Germany, workers were not immune to the national sentiments that were widespread in the rest of the population. Socialist party members received the same impressions from school, the army (if they served), and popular culture as nonsocialists did. The educated elite of the party leadership in both countries, itself often of bourgeois extraction, was far more likely to have the opportunity to experience the reality of international socialism, meeting like-minded socialist intellectuals at international congresses. The workers who formed the rank and file were more concerned with problems of everyday life; issues of international politics failed to hold their attention. Lacking the leisure or inclination to study conditions abroad for themselves, most workers were as prone to the stereotypes and misconceptions of the "hereditary enemy" as those who adhered to the middle-class parties.

The French and German socialist parties were the pillars of the Second International before 1914. In theory, socialists in both countries subscribed to the theory of international cooperation among members of the working classes. The parties were thus officially committed to working against militaristic policies of their respective governments. Patriotism was not unknown among socialists. However, in deliberate contrast to the pugnacious nationalism of the right, socialist patriotism, as described by Jean Jaurès or August Bebel, was intended as a benign cultural pride.[3] True patriotism, according to theorists of the left, complemented socialism, since the nation was the unit of political life and the means of cultural expression for the working classes.[4]

In spite of such idealism, patriotism *tout court* influenced socialists in both countries. On this issue, as on others, socialism was hampered by its own success. Socialist parties had developed in the space of a few decades from oppressed, semi-conspiratorial groups operating virtually underground to major political movements. As these parties became vast establishments with numerous vested interests, it was inevitable that they became more conservative, more bureaucratic, and perhaps more "bourgeois" in their opinions, for there was now much more at stake than a rudimentary party organization. The association of the parties with the more moderate trade unions also tended to temper calls for a revolutionary overthrow of the existing order. Instead, attention shifted to short-term goals such as concessions regarding wages, hours, working conditions, and the like from employers and bourgeois governments. This tendency went hand in hand with the development of reformist wings in the socialist parties of both countries. The temptation was to participate, at least tacitly, in bourgeois governments—to wring reforms out of the system rather than to overthrow it entirely. As workers came to have a greater share in the established order, revolutionary antipatriotism was bound to cool. The cherished theory of the international solidarity of the workers persisted, but it was parting company with reality. National rivalries were as likely to influence the thinking of the socialist rank and file as they did that of nonsocialists. In many ways, the differences in style between the French and German socialist parties additionally reflected and reinforced preconceived notions of each other's national characteristics.

The Social Democratic Party of Germany (SPD) was a formidable organization by 1912, when it emerged as the largest party in the Reichstag. It was the biggest, best-disciplined, and most influential party in the Second International. Under the capable leadership of August Bebel and Wilhelm Liebknecht, it had weathered many difficult years of oppression and emerged seemingly triumphant. Patient organizational work had built a strong party apparatus that drew increasing support from Germany's working classes.[5] The growth of the SPD coincided with a period of phenomenal industrial expansion in Germany, when economic growth brought about an unprecedented multiplication of the urban working class and a corresponding upsurge in SPD membership. However, Germany's increasing wealth also contributed to a greater prosperity and sense of well-being among German workers. The greater satisfaction felt by workers with their lot inevitably tended to assuage the revolutionary urge. In addition, ever more workers were employed in the armaments industry, and particularly in the building of the new battle fleet that was meant to force Britain to recognize German ambitions. The revisionists of the SPD, whose opinions on the prospects and desirability of revolution more accurately reflected those of the majority of the workers than did those of a Rosa Luxemburg or a Karl Liebknecht, sought to challenge some of the basic notions of socialist internationalism and antimilitarism. They hoped to wrest control of the party from a leadership they saw as increasingly moribund and rivals they considered dangerously radical, and to transform policies they saw as excessively doctrinaire.

There were two major theoretical journals of German socialism before the war, the orthodox *Die Neue Zeit* and the revisionist *Sozialistische Monatshefte*. One is struck in reading both these journals by the paucity of articles on France and the problems of Franco-German relations before 1914. One searches in vain for a prominent representative of the SPD who shared Jaurès's devotion to the long-term task of forging understanding between the two peoples. Most of the articles on France in both journals took a critical stance toward the fragmentation and indiscipline of French socialism. It appears that German socialist writers were more interested in comparing the organizational efforts of the two parties and finding the French socialists wanting rather than in devising a realistic strategy for maintaining peace. There was a deep-rooted impression that the SPD was the leading European socialist party, and that the French should follow its example and fall in behind it. The major party organ, *Vorwärts*, and the large regional socialist papers such as the *Leipziger Volkszeitung* were strictly orthodox and maintained an earnest (and dull) tone on Franco-German affairs, with little in-depth analysis of the difficulties between the two countries.[6]

The revisionist wing in German Social Democracy was represented by Eduard Bernstein and his followers, who founded the journal *Sozialistische Monatshefte* to develop and disseminate their theories of evolutionary socialism. Bernstein was strongly influenced by the example of British economic and political development, and was less familiar with conditions in France. Bernstein himself naturally favored French socialism's reformist tendency, known as "Millerandism" after Alexandre Millerand, who in 1899 became the first European socialist to serve in a national government.[7] At the same time, like many other German socialists, Bernstein was critical of what he perceived as the general indiscipline and chaotic organization of French socialism. In other matters, Bernstein showed an idiosyncratic view of French affairs. He labeled the anticlerical policies of the Waldeck-Rousseau and Combes governments, which included the law of associations, the laicization of schools, and the law for the separation of Church and state, a French "Culturkampf," and actually expressed sympathy for the Church, fighting for its timeless ideals against the secular interests of the moment. (Perhaps this was a reflection of his own struggles against the doctrinaire SPD leadership.)[8] In spite of all this, and the generally more "patriotic" trend among his revisionist colleagues, Bernstein was a staunch internationalist. Other reformists criticized France in ways that seemed strikingly similar to more bourgeois critiques.

The reformist wing of the Social Democrats also tended to be more hospitable toward those colleagues known as "social imperialists." The latter supported German expansion overseas, and by extension rivalry with other great powers, because they believed that the German working classes stood to benefit from the policy of *Weltpolitik*. The huge number of workers employed producing armaments could hardly disagree.[9] Some revisionist theorists shared the opinion prevalent among commentators further to the right that France's declining population and stagnant industry made it unworthy of great power status.[10] There was, however, an invisible limit that most party stalwarts were unwilling to cross. When a prominent socialist economist and supporter of Bernstein, Gerhard Hildebrand, attempted to argue in a controversial book that the SPD should embrace the program of imperialism and national expansion, he was expelled from the party.[11] It was far less simple to expel expansionist sentiments from the minds of the rank and file, however. At the end of 1912, the French socialist Charles Andler published a series of articles criticizing what he saw as a rising tide of chauvinism, perhaps even a procapitalist trend, in the SPD. The suspicion grew among French socialists that their German comrades might not be able to resist the clarion call of their government in the event of war.[12]

One final issue that had important ramifications for the attitude of the SPD toward attempts at Franco-German reconciliation was the Franco-Russian alliance. French socialists, Jaurès in particular, criticized the partnership of republican France with reactionary tsarist Russia. Nevertheless, the reality of the alliance tended to have more weight with German socialists than any French criticisms of it did. German socialists were almost unanimous in their hatred and fear of tsarist Russia, the bastion of reaction and Slavdom. The German left despised Russia not just for its harsh repression of revolutionaries, but also because German socialists had inherited Marx's own traditional German disdain for the Slavs. Thus, the looming menace of invasion from the east by Cossack hordes could chill the heart of even the staunchest German proponent of internationalism. When war finally broke out in 1914, the German government, well aware of such fears, successfully played the trump card of the Russian "steamroller" to bring German socialists obediently to its side. Thus, the SPD, with the exception of a few isolated voices of protest such as that of Rosa Luxemburg, lent its support to a war deliberately begun by Germany with an invasion of France, leaving their French "comrades" little choice but to fight.

It is interesting to note that several French observers developed a theory remarkably similar to the thesis developed by the West German historian Fritz Fischer in the late 1950s and early 1960s.[13] According to Fischer, the foreign policy of Imperial Germany was part of a "grab for world power" engineered by the country's élites, in particular the large landowners and the great industrialists. This expansionist policy was conceived first and foremost as a response to the rising menace of socialism at home. As such, the German Empire's decision to force a war represented, in Fischer's view, a "flight forward" (*Flucht nach vorn*) from the specter of revolution at home. Seen from France, the growth of the SPD may indeed have presented a vision of a looming threat of revolution in Germany, or at the very least an electoral victory leading inevitably to sweeping reform and government from below. How ironic it is then to see how deferential German socialists proved to be to their social superiors when the hour of war came. One French expert on military affairs correctly predicted that on the first day of mobilization, the German socialists would fall into ranks to shoot at their "comrades" on the other side.[14]

French, in contrast to German, socialists had been divided among several different parties. In addition, anarchism had a more substantial following in France than in Germany. Nevertheless, in the years before World War I, the Parti Socialiste (PS), or Section Française de l'Internationale Ouvrière (SFIO), was emerging as the dominant force in French socialism under the leadership of Jean Jaurès. A highly cultivated graduate of the prestigious Ecole Normale Supérieure, Jaurès had written a dissertation (in Latin) on the origins of German socialism. He also spoke German, though precisely how well is not clear. He consistently expressed a deep admiration for German Social Democracy and its discipline and organizational success, and his articles in *L'Humanité* provided perhaps the most extensive coverage of Franco-German relations in any European socialist journal or newspaper. In his well-known book *L'armée nouvelle*, Jaurès argued that the army of the future should resemble its forebears of the French revolution in being a national militia in which citizen soldiers would make up for a lack of professional acumen with a surfeit of patriotic zeal. Jaurès's conception of the ideal army was in direct contrast to that of the military professionals, who pushed for an increase in the number of years of military training from two to three so as to increase the size of the standing army by half. This measure passed in the spring of 1913 in spite of the strong opposition of Jaurès and many Radicals.

The French socialists, and Jaurès in particular, were somewhat more active in their pursuit of antiwar measures than their German counterparts. Certainly they tended to take the theory of the general strike in the event of war far more seriously. *L'Humanité*, the leading socialist newspaper in France, tended to follow Jaurès's line in supporting a French rapprochement with Germany and calling for a general strike in the event of war.[15] The French government was sufficiently alarmed by the specter of a mobilization crippled by large-scale socialist resistance to take elaborate precautions, including the formulation of a list of prominent socialists and antiwar activists to be arrested in the event of war, the infamous Carnet B.[16] This plan was never implemented, as the actual circumstances of the war's outbreak rendered moot any of French socialism's plans to stop "capitalist" aggression. Defense of the *patrie* was recognized as a duty by the workers, who in the event went to war equally determined if less fervently patriotic than their German "comrades."

One of Jaurès's more strident critics was the radical anarchist and antimilitarist Gustave Hervé, whose major base of support was among the workers of the Paris region. Hervé denied that the working class could feel national attachments of any sort. In a celebrated book titled *Leur patrie* (1905) and subsequent books and pamphlets, Hervé argued that the only "country" demanding the allegiance of the workers was the international socialist movement. Hervé had high expectations that in the event of an international crisis a general strike could sufficiently paralyze mobilization so that war would be impossible. French and German critics of Hervé, however, objected that it was unreasonable to expect the proletariat to have more influence under the extraordinary circumstances of the outbreak of war than they had in peacetime.[17] If the socialist parties of France and Germany were unprepared to seize power in the calm of peace, according to these critics, they would be even less able to do so given the uncertain events surrounding an outbreak of hostilities. Hervé also cut a poor figure at national and international socialist conferences, where he was usually bested in debates with the likes of Jaurès. In the event, no effort was even made by the socialists of either country at the outbreak of war to prevent mobilization. It is an open question whether Jaurès would have tried to stop the war had he not been assassinated, or whether he would have thrown himself into the effort of national defense.

There were numerous attempts to address worsening relations between France and Germany at international socialist conferences, as well as during the periodic war scares, during the period 1905–1914. Nevertheless, these efforts usually had limited success in achieving lasting understandings. The SPD showed a lack of commitment to an active policy of international arbitration and disarmament, and one result was a growing distrust of the German socialists by their French counterparts. The refusal of the SPD leadership, particularly that of the veteran socialist leader (and son of a career noncommissioned officer!) August Bebel, to tie its hands by a binding agreement on a general strike in the event of war inevitably caused French socialists to question the intentions of German socialists. The distinction between "offensive" and "defensive" war may have been clear to the Germans, but was hardly so to socialist representatives of other countries.[18] French critics such as Andler and Hervé were quick to point out the discrepancies between theory and reality among the German socialists.

The official stand of the Second International on questions of war and militarism was the resolution of the Stuttgart Congress of 1907. The debate that preceded the resolution revealed many of the splits in the International that ultimately proved fatal. The eloquence of Jaurès failed to persuade the SPD leadership of the necessity of a common policy to avert the threat of war. The final draft of the resolution merely states: "The International is not able to lay down the exact form of working class action against militarism at the right place and time, as this naturally differs in different countries. But its duty is to strengthen and co-ordinate the endeavours of the working classes against the war as much as possible."[19]

Hervé, saying that the German socialists feared power and prison equally, accused the German delegation of being subject to "a discipline of death," and concluded that "our internationalism is merely a sham for the proletariat."[20] The appearance in 1911 of Hildebrand's book describing a revisionist outlook on socialist foreign policy contributed to the mounting uncertainty among French socialists regarding their German "comrades." Hervé himself became increasingly anti-German, and after the outbreak of war he swung over to a radical nationalist stance.[21] Nevertheless, even Jaurès, in spite of all his speeches and writings promoting peace and rapprochement with Germany, vowed at the national congress of Nancy, shortly before Stuttgart, that the working classes would do their duty if France were invaded and criticized those of his comrades who were more prudent about the course the Germans should follow than the Germans were themselves.[22] Such utterances would hardly have come from someone who was committed to peace at any price.

The Right

Increasing disillusionment with the ideals of positivism and universal progress that had shaped much of nineteenth-century European thought, in conjunction with the rise of a socialist internationalism that appeared to threaten the existing order, contributed to a strong upsurge of nationalist sentiment in both France and Germany in the years before World War I. Nationalist ideology was relatively easy to grasp, and made virtues out of passive qualities such as birth, language, and "stability," the latter usually being associated with rootedness to the soil (*Bodenständigkeit*). Peasants, in particular, were more likely to identify with nationalist thought than with socialism, which was the preferred political creed of the industrial masses of the cities. In nationalist theory, the enemy of the nation is a necessary adjunct to the development of a national consciousness. In particular, the notion of the hereditary enemy is a corollary to the theory that the nation is rooted in the blood and soil of a particular place through millennia of development. German national consciousness as a mass phenomenon began to take shape only after 1870, and some have argued that the same was true for France.[23] Whatever the case, the antagonism between the two countries did much to shape nationalist thought in both France and Germany. The specter of a hostile Germany served to unite a French nation that included provincials of many different ethnic backgrounds, while the notion of the French hereditary enemy (*Erbfeind*) became part and parcel of the evolving German national mythology. Of course, the values that might normally be considered "patriotic" in one's own national context often appeared as naked chauvinism, militarism, and aggression when displayed by the enemy.

While the nationalists represented numerically one of the smallest portions of the political spectrum (with the possible exception of the pacifists), their mythologies of the adversary exerted perhaps the greatest influence. The style of nationalism was different in each country, though both took 1870 as a point of departure. German nationalists were brash, basking in the glory of victory, though plagued by an underlying uncertainty about Germany's future role and a nervous defensiveness about European resentment of their newfound strength. French nationalists tended to be more inward-looking, seeking explanations for the defeat of 1870, worried by the relative economic and demographic "stagnation" of France vis-à-vis Germany, but more confident about their country's rightful position in the world. Nevertheless, there was deep pessimism concerning the threat posed by a growing German industrial power. What each had in common was an ongoing enmity toward the other, varying in intensity but definitely on the increase after the turn of the century. Right-wing thinkers were increasingly likely to view crises in Franco-German relations as evidence of the eternal malice of the enemy, for which the only solution was armed conflict. Nationalist rhetoric tended to percolate into much of the popular press, such as the large Parisian dailies, and many of the major German newspapers.[24]

The French right was in some disarray after the Dreyfus Affair, when it appeared that its adversaries had won a crushing victory. The pre-eminence of the Dreyfusards, however, was shaken when it was discovered in 1906 that the government of the radically anticlerical Emile Combes was keeping tabs on Catholic army officers by way of spies recruited from Masonic lodges. After 1905, nationalist thought was increasingly influential, at least among French intellectuals and students. A small but vocal minority demonstrated an increasing hostility toward Germany.[25] According to two observers of the student scene, professors at the Sorbonne were more and more reluctant to speak positively of German methods of research and scholarship, for fear of being heckled by their anti-German students.[26]

The German bogey was useful not only as a foil for French virtues, but as a weapon against adversaries at home. French royalists found a welcome alternative to the corruption and cynicism of parliamentary politics in the apparent strength, stability, and decisiveness of the Prussian monarchy, at least until doubts began to form among many French observers about Wilhelm II's leadership abilities. By contrast, the French republic seemed weak, divided, and unable to follow a consistent foreign policy, while the army was disgraced in the aftermath of the Dreyfus Affair.[27] The men of Berlin, at least at a distance, appeared to offer a model of hard realism not restrained by a puerile ideology of liberal parliamentarism.[28] French pacifists and socialists were accordingly traitors or dupes, taken in by what many French right-wing observers believed to be the conscious playacting of their German counterparts.

In spite of their praise of some German virtues, French nationalists could also catalogue German vices when it served their purposes. Charles Péguy, in an essay that remained unpublished at his death, contrasted the

French spirit of chivalry with the German desire for domination—the one race combated while the other conquered.[29] According to Maurice Barrès, the greater discipline and efficiency of the Germans was purchased at the expense of individual initiative: "A German soldier always seems like a beaten dog."[30] The French soldier, by contrast, though not temperamentally suited to brutish discipline, would overcome the enemy through intelligence and *élan*. For Barrès, the qualities that made a Frenchman—urbanity, generosity, and altruism—were well out of reach of the barbarous, gauche, rude, and drunken German.[31] Barrès's novels reflect his belief that race was determined by an age-old identity with the soil of a particular place, and could not be acquired by means of assimilation or education. In general, authors such as Bainville, Barrès, and Péguy portrayed the French as guided by free will, which makes men and forms societies, while the Germans allowed themselves to be bound by the supposed laws of continuity and universal determinism, the intellectual equivalents of the mindless discipline they preferred.[32]

Many French right-wing intellectuals shared an essential pessimism about the future of France. While German population and industrial strength increased, France appeared to stagnate by comparison. It seemed clear to French cultural pessimists that, in spite of French virtues, Berlin must one day supplant Paris as the center of Europe. Nevertheless, it was important to struggle against the inevitable, for the spirit of chivalry demanded the courage of combat against superior strength and numbers. Just as the Roman legions had resisted the Teutonic onslaught to the best of their ability, the modern heroes of the Latin race would hold out against the Germanic flood even if the empire collapsed in decay around them.[33]

If French nationalists were alarmed at the growth of German power and determined to oppose it at all costs, German nationalists were frustrated that France, a nation apparently in decline, remained a world power with a large colonial empire. The growing conviction that German *Weltpolitik* was failing to bear fruit, and that Germany did not have its fair share of the colonial spoils, contributed to the hostility of German nationalists toward France. Nevertheless, there was a tendency to underestimate France in German nationalist writings, where more and more Britain was viewed as the primary enemy. This was partly a legacy of Germany's crushing victory over France in 1870, and lingered well into World War I. It has long been debated how much influence nationalist organizations such as the Alldeutscher Verband (Pan-German League) had on the ruling circles of Imperial Germany. In any case, it seems clear that Germany was more willing to go to war to right what was perceived as an inequitable balance in the international system.

Right-wing observers in Germany who wrote about France before 1914 repeatedly returned to the theme of the disparity in size between France and Germany's colonial empires. Heinrich Claß, head of the Pan-German League, noted that France was "internally unhealthy" (*innerlich ungesund*) but nevertheless had succeeded in widening its sphere of influence.[34] Claß' "solution" to the French threat was a war to defeat France once and for all, so that no future danger could threaten from that quarter. Friedrich von Bernhardi, in his popular book *Germany and the Next War*, agreed: "France must be so completely crushed that she can never again come across our path."[35] Bernhardi feared that the primary aim of French colonial policy was material and military superiority over Germany, partly by way of recruitment of an African army.

It is difficult to determine exactly how much of an echo nationalist rhetoric found in the population at large, but it achieved a high visibility at home, and could cause substantial concern abroad. There was a tendency in both France and Germany, not confined to right-wing extremists, to view the writings and utterances of nationalist individuals and groups in the opposite country as typical of public opinion and generally to overestimate the influence of French and German radical nationalists on their respective governments. French observers accordingly focused on articles appearing in the journal of the Pan-German League, the *Alldeutsche Blätter*, for proof of Germany's evil designs, while Germans sought evidence of French desires for revanche in the pages of *Action Française*.[36] Georges Bourdon, in an extremely hostile chapter of his book on contemporary Germany, described the Pan-German as a kind of evil troll: "The Pan-German's complexion is yellow, his lips dry, and he sees everything through a sea-green bilious medium. He does not live on the heights; he avoids the light, and from his hiding-place he picks to pieces treaties, exercises his malign influence on newspaper articles, pores over maps, measures angles, and traces with gloating eagerness the lines of frontiers."[37] The publications of the extreme right seemed to confirm the worst fears of the opposite nation, regardless of the narrow political influence these groups actually exercised on the conduct of foreign affairs or the skepticism that greeted their angry outbursts in their own countries.

And Everyone in Between

The broad political "center" in both France and Germany during these years tended to be fragmented in its views on almost every conceivable issue. Representatives of the bourgeois parties did, however, share one thing: a general lack of interest in foreign affairs outside of periods of crisis. Those more to the left, corresponding to the Radicals in France or the Progressives in Germany, might have some ideas in common with the pacifists or socialists, while those on the right commonly had more nationalist leanings. Most tended to share a certain "common-sense" approach to difficulties between the two countries. Nevertheless, there were distinct differences between the groups in France and Germany. In Germany, the Progressives, aware of the shortcomings of the constitution of the German

Empire, admired France's political institutions and hoped for the development of a more democratic regime in Germany. However, liberalism had failed to take deep root in Germany following its defeat in the revolution of 1848 and Bismarck's unification of Germany "from above," and divisions among German liberals, as well as fear of the socialist threat, tended to derail efforts at reform. The German Center Party, the political voice of German Catholics, faced certain obstacles to a more friendly policy toward France. The Center had been very sensitive to charges of being antipatriotic ever since the *Kulturkampf*, when charges of ultramontanism had been leveled against German Catholics. At the same time, there was widespread distaste among Center Party adherents for the French anticlerical legislation, and a certain anti-French tone predominated in the party newspaper *Germania*. Nevertheless, the Center would probably have supported friendlier relations with France that did not necessitate a sacrifice of German honor. The National Liberals, located more to the right of the political center, faced a choice of economic interests. This party was the dominant political voice of large industrialists, who benefited a great deal from increased armaments orders. However, they also stood to benefit from the trade agreements that would probably accompany a Franco-German rapprochement. While any such rapprochement would have required careful negotiation, it was possible that it could have found enough support to achieve passage in the German Reichstag.

Prime Minister Joseph Caillaux's attempt to achieve an understanding between France and Germany in the wake of the Agadir crisis marked a belated, and unsuccessful, return to a policy of pragmatic resolution of the Franco-German antagonism. Caillaux's many critics branded him as "pro-German," and he suffered a political setback as a result. Nevertheless, support for such a course was not insubstantial in France. A number of observers in both France and Germany already saw a continental European economic union as a necessity in the face of current or potential competition from the United States, Russia, and the British Empire. In France a small, though not insignificant, group of politicians, businessmen, and publicists sought a rapprochement with Germany. In addition, many members of the *parti colonial*, a loose grouping that represented colonial interests in the Assembly, believed that the colonies were more important than Alsace-Lorraine, though of course it was politically inexpedient after 1900 to express a preference for overseas territories over the lost provinces. The alternative of rapprochement seemed to offer the advantages of recognizing the realities of the existing international balance of power, particularly in the wake of Russia's disastrous defeat in its war against Japan, as well as providing a counterweight to France's traditional enemy, Britain. This group naturally elicited a favorable response from some German circles, but it was difficult to pursue an open process of improving relations given the predominantly anti-German trend in the French press. While many of these partisans of a Franco-German rapprochement considered themselves "pragmatists," they realized that such a rapprochement was an increasingly hard sell.

The liberal German political scientist Hermann Fernau published a remarkable book in 1914 entitled *French Democracy: Sociopolitical Studies from France's Cultural Workshop.*[38] Fernau's book ran astonishingly against the grain of prevalent German opinion, particularly in light of its year of publication. Fernau's very positive evaluations of France's political institutions were matched by a scathing critique of their German counterparts. Fernau considered France to be the most highly developed modern state. He bemoaned the declining respect for the individual in Germany, which he saw as partly a result of high birth rates.[39] Perhaps most importantly, Fernau argued that what was perceived by many German observers as French "decadence" was actually the outcome of enlightened social and political progress, whereby everything patriotic, warlike, holy, honorable, pious, virtuous, and dutiful was turned on its atavistic head.[40] The unfettered criticism of established political, social, and cultural institutions taken for granted in France was precisely what was most needed in Germany. It is difficult to overemphasize how rare this kind of heresy was in Germany before World War I.

It is possible that French and German adherents of classical liberal economic theory could have jointly developed a workable conception of liberal internationalism based on free trade. However, liberalism was in steep decline throughout Europe by the turn of the century, and at any rate had never had the ascendancy in France and Germany that it had once achieved in Britain. German liberalism was particularly weakened by its association with Bismarck's *Machtpolitik* in the foundation of the German Empire. The era before World War I was not one to favor compromise, particularly in the realm of international affairs. The dominant notions of Social Darwinism and *Realpolitik* were the foundations of a world view that favored the *lex talonis* over the liberal concepts of free trade, balance of power, and the settlement of conflicts by international congresses. The increasing reliance on the threat of force as the ultimate arbiter in international affairs eventually made recourse to war seem inevitable.

Most of the major newspapers and journals in both countries during this period belonged more or less in the large center of the political spectrum. The quality of the press varied enormously, from respectable reviews catering to the educated middle and upper classes to the more sensationalistic popular press with its mass-market circulation. There was less variation in the presentation of the image of the opposite nation in France and Germany than one might expect in such a large cross-section of the press. Few journals and papers espoused the theoretical internationalism of the socialist press. However, many more seemed open to influence from the nationalist press. This was especially true of the large-circulation dailies, such as the "quatre grands" in France (*Le Journal, Le Petit Journal, Le Petit Parisien, Le Matin*). However, even the more prominent papers such as *Le Temps* or the *Berliner Tageblatt* could take a nationalistic stance in times of crisis. Only the largest papers could maintain foreign correspondents in Berlin or Paris, while the rest relied on the papers of the capitals or on press bureaux like Agence Havas.[41]

There were several journals in both countries that, though having relatively small circulations, exercised considerable influence in constructing the image of the opposite country. The *Revue des Deux Mondes* in France and the *Deutsche Revue* in Germany, both increasingly concerned with the problems of Franco-German relations after the turn of the century, tended to become more hostile in their evaluations after 1905.[42] Maximilian Harden, editor of *Die Zukunft* and one of the most influential publicists of Wilhelmine Germany, could be ferocious in his articles on France, though he spoke excellent French and hoped that France would align with Germany.[43] A special place in the construction of the image of the enemy was occupied by humor magazines and satirical journals, such as *L'Assiette au Beurre* and *Simplicissimus*. The caricatures that such journals published were often far more effective in fixing ideas about the opposite nation in the minds of their readers than the articles they contained.

The press in Germany was less centered on the impressions and attitudes of the capital than that in France. Nevertheless, as the years passed a certain similarity of opinion toward France emerged in many of these papers, though the style of presentation may have differed. Coverage of foreign affairs in the *Neue Preußische Zeitung*, the newspaper catering to the conservative Prussian landowners, was dominated by Theodor Schiemann, a Baltic German who was more concerned with Russia than France, which he considered a second-rate power. The *Norddeutsche Allgemeine Zeitung* and the *Kölnische Zeitung* had ties to the German Foreign Office and became increasingly hostile toward France. Other more liberal dailies such as the *Frankfurter Zeitung* also assumed a more anti-French tone, while the *Münchner Neueste Nachrichten* dismissed French claims with its characteristic humorous style. In the last years of peace, it was difficult to find a major newspaper in Germany outside the left that entertained warm feelings toward France.

The Pacifist Alternative

The pacifist movement in Europe faced almost insurmountable obstacles to the propagation of its message in the years before 1914. Long-established habits of thought worked against the establishment of permanent bodies for peaceful arbitration of conflicts between countries. Most statesmen, industrialists, and intellectuals accepted war as an inevitability, or even as a positive experience in the life of nations. The amount of coverage, most of it very positive, devoted to military matters in the daily press of the period is astonishing. In spite of vociferous critics, the military in both France and Germany was held in high regard by most of the population. The fact that there had not been a major war between European great powers for a generation helped to turn war into an abstraction, if not a fantasy, for the general population, and few outside of the realm of military specialists, or narrow circles of poets and artists, were able or willing to grasp the potential horrors of a new conflict. Few shared the pessimism of the eccentric author of a book about prophecies of the imminent downfall of the Hohenzollern dynasty, who predicted that a war was approaching "from which the map of Europe, reddened by appalling slaughter, will emerge transformed and utterly unrecognizable."[44] In order for their message to have any resonance, pacifists had to overcome popular indifference, nationalist enmities, and outmoded notions of the romanticism of war.

There were two options open to pacifists working to improve relations between France and Germany. Either they could support efforts in favor of world peace and disarmament, as manifested by the Hague conferences of 1899 and 1907, or they could work for Franco-German reconciliation within the traditional diplomatic framework of a balance of power. Most practitioners of pacifism considered themselves "realistic" and patriotic, and tended to favor the second option. Many German observers suspected that the Hague conferences, summoned at the suggestion of the tsar Nicholas II, were merely cynical ploys to slow the arms race so that Russia would not fall too far behind.[45] A Franco-German rapprochement seemed to most pacifists a more promising solution to the danger of a continental war than the chimera of eternal peace. The time when such a reconciliation between France and Germany appeared closest at hand was during the Boer War (1899–1902). Franco-British relations had been strained as a result of the standoff on the upper Nile at Fashoda in 1898, which ended with a French withdrawal, while there was widespread indignation in Germany over Britain's high-handed behavior in South Africa.[46] However, the opportunity slipped by and instead France achieved a successful rapprochement with Britain at the initiative of Foreign Minister Théophile Delcassé.

While socialist attempts to overcome the prevailing *Feindbild* were restrained by the gap between theorists and the rank and file, pacifists were hampered by the fact that their movement tended to attract only a narrow following, largely confined to a small segment of the middle class. Although increasing tensions after 1905 contributed to a sense of urgency in the international pacifist movement, pacifist organizations were unable to attract the mass following that was necessary for the success of their efforts in either France or Germany. In Germany, the Verband für Internationale Verständigung, founded by Alfred Fried in 1911, was intended as an élite organization that would impose unity on the peace movement and work directly with political leaders.[47] Unfortunately, the man chosen by Fried to head the Verband, Otfried Nippold, was unpopular with local chapters of the peace movement. In France, the peace movement was ably represented by the former prime minister Léon Bourgeois and the deputy Paul Henri Benjamin, baron d'Estournelles de Constant, a grand-nephew of Benjamin Constant and founder of Conciliation internationale (Society for International Conciliation).[48] The leading French and German pacifist organizations joined forces in 1913 to publish the short-lived *Veröffent-lichungen des Verbandes für Internationale Verständigung*, which ceased publication the following year with the sharp drop in demand for peace.[49]

Prominent pacifists attempted to present projects for Franco-German rapprochement as exercises in enlightened self-interest. Most tended to see the arms race between France and Germany as a crushing burden and a distraction from more pressing problems—in the words of one observer, "a stupid, unequal, criminal duel."[50] Many considered an alliance of the "cultured nations" (France, Germany, and Britain) a necessity in the face of competition from the Slavs, the United States, or, in d'Estournelles' case, the "Yellow Peril."[51] In a speech given in the upper house of the Prussian parliament, d'Estournelles predicted that a successful war of revanche by France could only result in deeper bitterness between the two countries.[52] Some German pacifists argued that Germany could follow a course of expansion without war, by way of a shrewd manipulation of existing alliances.[53] Nevertheless, patriotism carried great weight even among advocates for peace, and French and German pacifists tended to support their respective governments during diplomatic crises, such as the confrontations over Morocco.[54]

In spite of its prominent leadership, the Conciliation internationale failed to attract a large following. The years of its greatest activity coincided with the period of greatest tension in relations among the great powers. Socialists were initially hostile to the pacifist organization, which officially stated that the development of capitalism would lead to world peace, and only began to support it in the last years before the war.[55] In Germany, pacifism failed to make much impression on either the masses or the educated upper middle classes, while in France it was difficult to appeal to the general public for recognition of a peace that would ratify the loss of Alsace-Lorraine.

The culmination of attempts by pacifists to bring about a rapprochement in Franco-German relations was the interparliamentary conference held in Bern in May 1913. The conference was called in response to the tensions caused by the Balkan Wars and the resultant army bills in France and Germany. Delegates from the French National Assembly and Senate and the Reichstag gathered for discussions of some of the major issues that separated the two countries. The French and German press covered the conference with some interest, and real hostility was largely limited to the right-wing press, which was quick to note the disproportionately large participation of socialist delegates. However, there was a sharp disparity between the number of French and German delegates (185 and 34, respectively), and the German delegation in particular was indeed largely composed of socialists. Given such an imbalance, the conference was doomed to failure. A similar conference in Basel the following spring drew much less interest and participation. Thus, the final efforts to achieve a pacifist solution to the Franco-German antagonism only served to accentuate further the gulf between the two countries.[56]

Conclusion

Each of the political tendencies outlined above influenced the formation of the image of the enemy in France and Germany before 1914. The nationalists, however, were most successful in transmitting their ideas to a larger public. The right's simple messages of national values concerning the land, the army, family, and religion were easier to grasp than the rationalized internationalism of the socialists, whose utopia was at any rate defined by class, and appealed to nostalgic visions of an idealized past. The reflexive patriotism and antisocialism of the middle-class parties in both countries made them an ideal breeding ground for mythologies of the enemy. The mainstream press in both France and Germany seemed to be more open to influence from the right than the left, and the cult of *patria* maintained its hold on the popular imagination. Even the socialist rank and file in both countries shared the patriotic impulses of the general population. Under such circumstances, those calling for a re-evaluation of the entrenched mythologies of the adversary found themselves isolated and discredited. Socialists and pacifists failed to work together even as they found themselves isolated by their common antiwar stance, while the right, on this issue at least, found a willing audience for its mythologies along the entire political spectrum. Both the French and the German right had discovered a way to appeal to a potential mass following, but the ideal conditions for the construction of enemies occurred only after World War I.

Notes

1. Paris: Félix Alcan, 1913, pp. 285–286.
2. This is the argument of Erwin Dörzbacher in *Die deutsche Sozialdemokratie und die nationale Machtpolitik bis 1914* (Gotha: Perthes, 1920).
3. Nicholas Stargardt, *The German Idea of Militarism: Radical and Socialist Critics, 1866–1914* (Cambridge: Cambridge University Press, 1994), p. 56.
4. A thorough, though uninspired work on attitudes toward war among French and German socialists is M. M. Drachkovitch, *Les socialismes français et allemand et le problème de la guerre 1870–1914* (Geneva: E. Droz, 1953).
5. The standard work on the SPD just before and during World War I is Carl Schorske, *German Social Democracy, 1905–1917: The Development of the Great Schism* (Cambridge: Harvard University Press, 1955); a somewhat more recent (and exhaustive) study is

Dieter Groh's *Negative Integration und revolutionärer Attentismus: Die deutsche Sozialdemokratie am Vorabend des Ersten Weltkrieges* (Frankfurt a. M.: Ullstein, 1973). The best history of the Second International remains James Joll's *The Second International 1889–1914* (New York: Harper and Row, 1966).

6. See Alex Hall, *Scandal, Sensation, and Social Democracy: The SPD Press and Wilhelmine Germany 1890–1914* (Cambridge: Cambridge University Press, 1977).

7. See, for example, his article "Zur jüngsten Entwicklung der französischen Socialdemokratie," *Sozialistische Monatshefte* (April 1902): 250–251.

8. "Der Culturkampf in Frankreich," *Sozialistische Monatshefte* (December 1904): 963.

9. Georges Haupt, *Socialism and the Great War: The Collapse of the Second International* (Oxford: Clarendon Press, 1972), pp. 35–36; Schorske, *German Social Democracy*, p. 244.

10. Richard Calwer, "Deutsch-französische Annäherung," *Sozialistische Monatshefte* 14, no. 2 (1908): 664.

11. Gerhard Hildebrand, *Sozialistische Auslandspolitik: Betrachtungen über die weltpolitische Lage anlässlich des Marokko-Streites* (Jena: E. Diederichs, 1911; a French translation was published the following year).

12. A very good account of the controversy over social imperialism can be found in Gilbert Ziebura, *Die deutsche Frage in der öffentlichen Meinung Frankreichs von 1911–1914* (Berlin-Dahlem: Colloquium Verlag, 1955), pp. 46–53. Andler published a collection of articles by social imperialists shortly after the end of World War I: *Le Socialisme impérialiste dans l'Allemagne contemporaine: dossier d'une polémique avec Jean Jaurès* (Brussels: Bossard, 1918). Andler, an Alsatian, was an excellent Germanist; German socialists with an equivalent expertise on France were rare.

13. See, for example, Bertrand Andrillon, *L'expansion de l'Allemagne: ses causes, ses formes, ses conséquences* (Paris: M. Riviere et cie., 1914), pp. 312–313; and René Pinon, *France et Allemagne 1870–1913* (Paris: Libraires-Editeurs, 1913), pp. 235–236. For Fischer's thesis, see his *Germany's Aims in the First World War* (London: Norton, 1967).

14. General Palat [pseud. of Pierre Lehautcourt], *L'alliance franco-allemande ou la guerre* (Paris: Librairie Chapelot, 1914), p. 108.

15. At one point when the paper was facing financial difficulties, Jaurès secured a grant of 25,000 francs from the German Social Democrats! See Harvey Goldberg, *The Life of Jean Jaurès* (Madison: University of Wisconsin Press, 1962), pp. 552–553, n. 127.

16. See Jean-Jacques Becker, *Le Carnet B: les pouvoirs publics et l'antimilitarisme avant la guerre de 1914* (Paris: Editions Klincksieck, 1973).

17. See Karl Kautsky, *Patriotismus und Sozialdemokratie* (Leipzig: Buchdruckerei Aktiengesellschaft, 1907), p. 5.

18. Jaurès, "Au Congrès d'Essen," *L'Humanité*, 28 September 1907; reprinted in *Œuvres* (Paris: Rieder, 1931–1939), vol. 5, pp. 173–174.

19. The resolution is reproduced in Joll, *The Second International*, pp. 173–174.

20. Jacques Droz, *Le socialisme allemand de 1869 à 1918* (Paris: Centre de Documentation Universitaire, 1970), p. 55; L. Gravereaux, *Les discussions sur le patriotisme et le militarisme dans les congrès socialistes* (Paris: G. Dussardier & P. Frank, 1913), p. 190. This moment probably marks the beginning of Hervé's move to the right.

21. Late in life, in 1935, Hervé had become sufficiently right-wing to publish a book entitled *C'est Pétain qu'il nous faut*. See Michel Winock, "Gustave Hervé: de la guerre sociale à la guerre," in Winock, *Nationalisme, antisémitisme et fascisme en France* (Paris: Editions du Seuil, 1990).

22. "Discours de Jaurès au congrès de Nancy" (13 August 1907), *Œuvres*, vol. 5.

23. See particularly Eugen Weber, *Peasants into Frenchmen: The Modernization of Rural France, 1870–1914* (Stanford: Stanford University Press, 1976).

24. For an interesting, and extensive, sampling of anti-French opinion in the mainstream German press during the years 1912 and 1913, see the collection of articles edited by the German pacifist Otfried Nippold, *Der deutsche Chauvinismus* (Berlin: W. Kohlhammer, 1913; 2nd ed. Bern, 1917).

25. John F. V. Keiger, *France and the Origins of the First World War* (New York: St. Martin's Press, 1983), pp. 75–76. Keiger believes that the "nationalist revival" in France has been exaggerated, and agrees with Jean-Jacques Becker that the dominant mood outside of Paris was "apatriotic."

26. Agathon [pseud. of Alexis de Tarde and Henri Massis], *Les jeunes gens d'aujourd'hui* (Paris: Plon-Nourrit, 1913), p. 29.

27. See, for example, Jacques Bainville, "Une machine bien montée," *Action Française* (23 December 1912), reprinted in *L'Allemagne*, vol. 1 (Paris: Librairie Plon, 1939), p. 51.

28. André Mévil, *La paix est malade* (Paris: Plon, 1914), pp. ix–x.

29. "Note conjointe sur M. Descartes et la philosophie cartésienne" (1914), in *Œuvres en prose, 1909–1914* (Paris: Gallimard, 1959), p. 1367.

30. Maurice Barrès, *Au service de l'Allemagne* (1905), in *L'Œuvre de Maurice Barrès*, vol. 6 (Paris: Au Club de l'Honnête Homme, 1966), p. 92.

31. Ibid., p. 113.

32. See Ernst Robert Curtius, *Maurice Barrès und die geistigen Grundlagen des französischen Nationalismus* (Hildesheim: Georg Olms, 1962; originally published 1921), p. 113ff.

33. This was the opinion of Jules Soury, professor of "physiological psychology" at the Sorbonne, who exercised a marked influence on Barrès. See Zeev Sternhell, *Maurice Barrès et le nationalisme français* (Paris: Armand Colin, 1972), pp. 256–259.

34. Heinrich Claß, *Wenn ich der Kaiser wär': Politische Wahrheiten und Notwendigkeiten* (Leipzig: Dieterich, 1913).

35. Friedrich von Bernhardi, *Germany and the Next War*, trans. by Allen H. Powles (New York: C.A. Eron, 1914), p. 105. The first German edition of Bernhardi's book appeared in 1912, and a French translation quickly followed.

36. See Paul Vergnet, *La France en danger: l'œuvre des pangermanistes, ce qu'il sont, ce qu'ils peuvent, ce qu'ils veulent* (Paris: La Renaissance du livre, 1913); Georges Bourdon, *The German Enigma: Being an Inquiry Among the Germans as to What They Think, What They Want, What They Can Do*, trans. by Beatrice Marshall (London: J.M. Dent and Sons, 1914), pp. 136–162; and Otfried Nippold, *Der deutsche Chauvinismus* (Berlin: W. Kohlhammer, 1913). The last is an excellent collection of articles appearing in the mainstream German press that demonstrates the widespread appeal of nationalist rhetoric in German papers in the last years before World War I.

37. Bourdon, *The German Enigma*, p. 136.

38. *Die französische Demokratie: Sozialpolitische Studien aus Frankreichs Kulturwerkstatt* (Munich: Duncker & Humblot, 1914).

39. Ibid., pp. 210–211.

40. Ibid., pp. 300–301.

41. See Klaus Wernecke, *Der Wille zur Weltgeltung: Aussenpolitik und Öffentlichkeit im Kaiserreich am Vorabend des Ersten Weltkrieges* (Düsseldorf: Droste, 1970), p. 8; Claude Bellanger, ed., *Histoire générale de la presse française* (Paris: Presses universitaires de France, 1976), vol. 3, p. 289.

42. See Norbert Ohler, *Deutschland und die deutsche Frage in der "Revue des Deux Mondes" 1905–1940: Ein Beitrag zur Erhellung des französischen Deutschlandbildes* (Frankfurt a. M.: Akademische Verlagsgesellschaft, 1973), p. 21.

43. See Harry F. Young, *Maximilian Harden, censor Germaniae: The Critic in Opposition from Bismarck to the Rise of Nazism* (The Hague: M. Nijhoff, 1959), pp. 157–159. The French certainly considered Harden a Gallophobe.

44. J.-H. Lavaur, *La fin de l'empire allemand: annoncée par plusieurs prophéties célèbres, précises et concordantes* (Paris: Editions pratiques et documentaires, 1913).

45. See Charles Guieysse, *La France et la paix armée: la Conférence de La Haye* (Paris: Librairie de "Pages libres," 1905).

46. See the pamphlet by Alfred Nossig, *Die Politik des Weltfriedens: Die deutsch-französische Annäherung und die Kontinentalunion* (Berlin: Hermann Walther, 1900).

47. See Roger Chickering, *Imperial Germany and a World without War: The Peace Movement and German Society, 1892–1914* (Princeton: Princeton University Press, 1976), p. 148ff. Chickering's book is the best work on German pacifism before 1914, and also contains an extensive chapter on pacifism in France.

48. The best source on the life and work of d'Estournelles de Constant is the exhaustive two-volume biography by Adolf Wild, *Baron d'Estournelles de Constant (1852–1924): Das Wirken eines Friedensnobelpreisträgers für die deutsch-französische Verständigung und europäische Einigung* (Hamburg: Fundament-Verlag Sasse, 1973). See also Laurent Barcelo, *Paul d'Estournelles de Constant: l'expression d'une idée européene* (Paris: Editions L'Harmattan, 1995).

49. *Conciliation internationale* had an American branch located in New York, the Society for International Conciliation, whose board members included Seth Low and Nicholas Murray Butler of Columbia University. Butler took a keen interest in Franco-German relations, and copies of many of the books and pamphlets referred to in this study, inscribed by their authors to Butler, can be found in the Columbia library.

50. Alfred Pevet, *Raisons historiques et actuelles d'un rapprochement franco-allemand* (Paris: Imp. de l'Emancipatrice, 1913), p. 33.

51. D'Estournelles noted the difficulties of bringing the blessings of Western culture to China: "One European nation is not enough to do it; the one has not enough inhabitants, the other not enough money; others lack experience." See "Frankreich und Deutschland," in *Veröffentlichungen des Verbandes für Internationale Verständigung*, vol. 5, from a speech given at the first meeting of the Verband in Heidelberg, 6 October 1912.

52. Paul Henri Benjamin, baron d'Estournelles de Constant, *Frankreich und Deutschland* (Berlin: W. Kohlhammer, 1913), pp. 18–19.

53. See Hans Plehn, *Deutsche Weltpolitik und kein Krieg* (Berlin: Puttkammer und Muhlbrecht, 1913), pp. 15–18.

54. Chickering, *Imperial Germany*, pp. 308–309.

55. Ibid., p. 265. Ironically, when certain French and German socialists began to view pacifism more favorably in the wake of the Agadir crisis, the nationalist press in both countries was able to taint pacifism with the additional brush of socialism.

56. For accounts of the conference, see Alwin Hanschmidt, "Die französisch-deutschen Parlamentarier-konferenzen von Bern (1913) und Basel (1914)," *Geschichte in Wissenschaft und Unterricht* 26, no. 6 (June 1975): 335–359; Chickering, *Imperial Germany*, pp. 279–282; and Albert Gobat, *La Conférence interparlementaire franco-allemande de Berne* (Bern: G. Grunau, 1913). Gobat was the director of the Swiss branch of the International Peace Bureau.

CONCLUSION

A fight in which we know with whom we have to do is a plain matter enough. But in the modern life-order, after a phase of temporary clearness, we are afflicted by the confusion of the fighting front. He who just now seemed our opponent, has become our ally. What in accordance with the objectivity of our voluntary expectations ought to be our adversary, joins forces with us; what seems really antagonistic, lays down its arms; what looked like a united front is divided against itself. All this occurs in a medley and amid a turbulent interchange. It makes my nearest neighbour my enemy and some one at the other side of the world my companion at arms.

Karl Jaspers, *Man in the Modern World*[1]

Because there never is the full experience of the myth in the present—myth, a mythical framework, always, by definition, emerges as a memory, as the retroactive reconstitution of something which, when it 'actually took place,' was simply a common vulgar play of passions?

Slavoj Žižek, *Did Somebody Say Totalitarianism?*
Five Interventions in the (Mis)use of a Notion[2]

The outbreak of war in 1914 opened a new era in Franco-German relations. The enormous suffering brought about by the war seemed to guarantee that the enmity between France and Germany would indeed become hereditary. The mobilization of virtually the entire population for total war in both countries was accompanied by frenzied propaganda that portrayed the adversary in the worst possible light. Nevertheless, the common catastrophe sowed the seeds of future reconciliation even as it seemed that the soil was forever poisoned.

As historians have noted, at the beginning of the war the Germans, faced with an array of adversaries, were hard put to select a primary enemy.[3] Much of the more venomous propaganda focused first on Russia,

---

Notes for this section appear on page 116.

and then on Britain. It was far more difficult to cast invaded France in the role of aggressor.[4] The French had no such uncertainties. The *boche* was the worst kind of barbarian, and his assault on France was an assault on civilization itself. The propaganda of both sides drew on prewar imagery, but the unprecedented loss of life occasioned by modern warfare quickly raised hatred to a new pitch. Nevertheless, in spite of the horrific nature of combat and the relentlessness of propaganda, the soldiers facing each other in the trenches often felt a greater bond with the adversaries who shared their suffering than with the ignorant civilians behind the lines. The real enemy seemed to be the war itself, as notions of patriotism were ground down by the relentless slaughter. Already during the war, discordant voices such as that of Henri Barbusse in *Le Feu* (1916) were less interested in demonizing Germans than portraying a world gone mad.

The war brought death in the most anonymous ways. The soldiers on opposite sides of no-man's land lived (and died) in close proximity, but rarely saw each other. Actual encounters often belied expectations. Jacques Rivière, who was a prisoner in Germany, recalled one of his guards, an old *Landsturm* man, who was called up for service at the front. Frightened at the prospect, he asked his prisoners for lessons in surrender.[5] Rivière also felt compelled to comment on the lack of sadism in the German character.[6] Such accounts flew in the face of wartime wisdom regarding the enemy. In a book published shortly after the war, Karl Lahm ruefully acknowledged that the Germans had seriously misjudged the French, noting that the Germans had been good salesmen in trading with France but bad psychologists in judging French character.[7]

Unfortunately, the spirit of reconciliation did not predominate after the war. Many Germans viewed the end of the conflict hopefully as a time for new beginnings, and expected a lenient peace based on President Woodrow Wilson's Fourteen Points. However, the stringent conditions of the Versailles Treaty, insisted on most strongly by France, came as a rude jolt to such optimistic expectations. The articles of the treaty called for an allied occupation of the Rhineland, French administration of the mineral-rich Saar territory, an enormous sum of reparations, and, worst of all, an admission of German war guilt. The treaty thus stood as major obstacle to Franco-German reconciliation: most Germans thought it excessively punitive and most French did not consider it sufficiently harsh at that time. The possibility that a normalization of relations between the two countries might occur seemed remote in the early 1920s.

Franco-German tensions reached their apogee in the Ruhr crisis of 1923. The government of Wilhelm Cuno in Germany opposed French claims for reparations by slowing delivery of coal from the Ruhr. The French responded by occupying the Ruhr and taking over administration of the mines themselves. The use of colonial troops in the occupation was especially vexing to many Germans, and became a symbol of French arrogance toward Germany. The occupation and the collective German policy of passive resistance were ruinous to both countries. France received considerably less coal from Germany than before the entry of its troops and its financial system was shaken by the costs of the occupation, while the German economy, already weakened by years of borrowing to finance the war effort, fell prey to runaway inflation. In the event, it was the Germans who gave in to French demands, but the dislocation caused to the French economy was a major factor in the devaluation of the French franc the following year. The Ruhr standoff left bitterness on both sides, but also a realization that alternatives to force were necessary if major economic upheavals were to be avoided and Europe as a whole were to recover its prewar stability.

The policy of rapprochement between France and Germany was most closely associated with Gustav Stresemann, who served as German foreign minister from 1924 until 1929. Stresemann, a National Liberal before the war and founder of the German People's Party (DVP), had been an outspoken proponent of an annexationist policy during the war. However, the experience of defeat and Germany's difficulties in the realms of economy and security since the end of the war convinced Stresemann that an understanding with France was necessary as the cornerstone of Franco-German, and by extension continental, prosperity. Germany's acceptance in 1924 of the Dawes Plan, which regulated payment of reparations, removed a major factor of uncertainty between France and Germany. Stresemann's opposite number in France, Prime Minister Aristide Briand, was also willing to pursue alternative methods of guaranteeing French security. The Treaty of Locarno, signed in October 1925, recognized Germany's western borders as permanent, and contributed to a greater feeling of security on the European scene. Stresemann, who in his very physical appearance seemed to many Frenchmen to be the image of the *boche* incarnate, made possible a new departure in Franco-German relations.[8] While Stresemann was probably seeking freedom of maneuver for a future readjustment of Germany's border with Poland, nevertheless his policy of building bridges between France and Germany produced impressive results and caused a significant lessening of tensions.[9]

Nevertheless, in spite of such progress, the achievement of deeper reconciliation was an uphill struggle. As one historian of the image of France in the Weimar Republic has noted, the notion of France as the "hereditary enemy" seemed more deeply rooted than ever in the wake of the Great War. The opinion was widespread among the German middle class that France sought to achieve mastery in Europe in spite of its inferior strength by way of guarantees from Britain and the United States, alliances with the new states of eastern Europe, and the use of colonial troops. At the same time, notions of French racial inferiority persisted in many German circles.[10] French fear of a resurgent Germany likewise remained a major obstacle to a complete normalization of relations. France faced the challenges of the postwar world with its population of young men much reduced by wartime casualties. Even the return of the lost provinces of Alsace and Lorraine turned out to be less than a cause for complete rejoicing. French authorities instituted a regime of passports and purge hearings that alienated many Alsatians and contributed to a movement for Alsatian autonomy in the 1920s.[11]

The late 1920s and early 1930s witnessed the beginnings of a cultural rapprochement that was a counterpart to the political. The passage of time allowed a more balanced view of the war to emerge, and the conviction that the struggle had been a senseless slaughter gained ground beyond a narrow range of artists and intellectuals in both France and Germany. Erich Maria Remarque's *All Quiet on the Western Front* (1927) was a best-seller in France as well as Germany, and marked the beginning of a flood of antiwar novels and memoirs. Even the coming to power of the Nazis in 1933 did not initially mark the sharp break in the trend that one might expect. Many French intellectuals expressed a spirit of conciliation toward Germany, while German writers on France during these years generally appeared sympathetic toward France and admiring of French culture. Hermann, Count Keyserling described the dissatisfaction felt about the war in both countries, noting that the German did not view defeat as personal responsibility (seeking fault elsewhere), while the Frenchman felt cheated even in victory.[12] Ernst Robert Curtius, in his influential book on French civilization, wrote wistfully of the attachment of the French to their national soil, which was in such sharp contrast to the *Wanderlust* of the German.[13] Curtius was also struck by France's greater attachment to the past and its cult of the dead, as one could witness at Père Lachaise or the Panthéon, as well as the site of the mutual slaughter at Verdun.[14] Such notions of stability and rootedness appealed to many Germans in a world fraught with uncertainty. Karl Tögel, in his book on "the real France," could write with sympathy that Verdun had reinforced French attachment to the pleasures of life and fear of a premature departure from the mortal coil. Tögel contrasted the conservative and static nature of the French with the stormy, creative, and dynamic German and his spirit of sacrifice, not unlike the difference between a parent and an adolescent child. For Tögel, it appeared that what the typical Frenchman wanted was a sense of security so that he could enjoy his weekend picnic of cold chicken and a bottle of wine in peace.[15] Karl Schwendemann, in his book on French culture, noted approvingly that France found its unity not in race, but in its concept of civilization, whereby not just Basques and Bretons, Flemings and Provençals, but also Arabs, Berbers, and black Africans could share the benefits of being French.[16]

The spirit of reconciliation found its echo in film. The director G. W. Pabst's film *Kameradschaft* of 1931 portrayed German miners coming to the rescue of their French counterparts in the wake of a mine disaster. Set shortly after World War I, the film ended on a hopeful note of reconciliation, in spite of its recognition of the persistence of hostility at the governmental level. Pabst's film found its French response in Jean Renoir's brilliant *Grand Illusion* of 1938, which portrayed the shared experiences of French prisoners of war and their German captors in the face of a senseless war. Unfortunately, Renoir's film expressed hopes of peace at exactly the wrong moment, as Hitler's Germany, no longer interested in a policy of conciliation, prepared to plunge Europe into a new war in the wake of the Munich conference.

One of the more disturbing tendencies on the intellectual scene in France was the emergence of apologists for the Nazis. In a book that first appeared as a series of articles written in 1933 and 1934, the prominent pacifist Jules Romains sought to play down the potential threat from Nazi Germany. Romains argued, all too reasonably, that it was unjust for Germany to remain disarmed among neighbors who were armed to the teeth, noting that the German man in the street supported rearmament but would think Hitler insane if he declared an offensive war.[17] Romains followed up with an article in which he explained that what such men as Hitler or Mussolini "wanted" in their deepest thoughts was never cast in bronze, explaining that the exigencies of changing circumstances worked against long-term plans. The only constant among such men was the will to personal grandeur. Romains railed against those who erred in seeing a grand plan behind a statesman's actions that would provide the key to dealing with him in the future.[18] Romains and other pacifists sought to make amends for past French harshness against Germany, and they feared the consequences of a new war so much that they were willing to do almost anything to avoid one. Unfortunately, many seriously misjudged the nature of Hitler and the Nazi regime. More egregious was the flirtation of elements on the French right that shared anti-Semitic and antidemocratic doctrines with Nazism, as well as the latter's virulent fear and hatred of the Bolsheviks.

Hitler considered France as little more than a hindrance to his ultimate plans for German expansion in the east. However, most Germans in the late 1930s still considered France a great military power. Hence, France's rapid defeat in the spring of 1940 came as a shock to both French and Germans. Nevertheless, Germany's victory over France failed to arouse rejoicing to the same extent as that which had greeted the outbreak of war in 1914, as the uncertainties of a continuing war weighed on the German public. Such doubts turned out to be well-founded. World War II ultimately shattered any remaining illusions that either country could continue to follow an independent course as a great power. Both France and Germany lost the war. Germany was occupied by its conquerors and partitioned, while France, no longer the powerful political factor it had been, was faced with continuing troubles at home and in its colonial empire.

The years immediately following World War II did not appear to be promising ones for ending hostility between France and Germany. In one of the most interesting books on Germany penned by a French author during these years, Robert d'Harcourt reflected on the seeming indifference of most Germans to the crimes of the Nazi regime, and their rejection of the notion of collective guilt. D'Harcourt wondered whether this was a sincere indifference or a defensive reflex before crushing historical reality.[19] D'Harcourt noted that Nazism had attempted to inspire both fear and pride among Germans. The Germans took pride in inspiring fear after the years of humiliation following World War I, yet even while causing their neighbors to fear they wondered why they were so hated. D'Harcourt believed that the terror the Germans unleashed was a compensatory reflex for a feeling of inferiority.[20] Whatever the case, the loathing the Germans had raised in the hearts of those who had been subject to Nazi rule made the prospect of cooperation unattractive to most French in the postwar period.

The initiative for reconciliation came from the top. The key figure in bringing France and Germany together was German chancellor Konrad Adenauer, who, though he had little experience of France, realized the two countries would have to work in unison to rebuild. As one historian has noted, Adenauer was strongly influenced by a succession of German-speaking French statesmen who likewise recognized the need for cooperation: André François-Poncet, Robert Schumann, Pierre Mendès-France, and Charles de Gaulle.[21] Beginning with agreements for common exploitation of coal and iron, the Franco-German partnership became the foundation of the European Community by the late 1950s. The friendship between Adenauer and de Gaulle in particular became a symbol of Franco-German cooperation. De Gaulle, formerly a staunch foe of Germany, recognized that France needed a special relationship with its old adversary in order to preserve its own voice in world affairs. Adenauer and de Gaulle, as well as Prime Minister de Gasperi of Italy, also shared an identity as political Catholics that aided their common effort to build the European Community. However, many in Germany distrusted de Gaulle's motives, and the Franco-German treaty of January 1963 was widely considered a dead letter in Germany because it displeased the Americans, whom most Germans recognized as their primary ally.

The 1960s witnessed a number of developments that changed the mutual perspectives of the two countries at deeper levels. The economic recovery brought increasing wealth to ordinary citizens in both France and Germany, and one consequence was a more widespread ability to travel to foreign countries. In addition, exchange programs brought together many French and German students and allowed them to see the opposite country firsthand. At the same time, the proliferation of mass media hastened the process of dissolving mental boundaries between the two countries. A new generation coming of age on both sides of the Rhine questioned many of the beliefs of their parents concerning the "hereditary enemy" and contributed to forming a vibrant international student culture. The role of the attempted assassination by right-wing fanatics of Rudi Dutschke, a popular student leader in Berlin, in precipitating the student uprising of

May 1968 in Paris, as well as the high visibility of Daniel Cohn-Bendit, a German Jew, as leader of the Parisian students, were testimony to a feeling of revolutionary solidarity that refused to recognize borders.

Nevertheless, misunderstandings persisted even in the face of increasing contacts. Jean Améry, an Austrian Jewish author who lived in exile in Belgium, wrote on the continuing influence of myths the French and Germans held of each other in the mid 1970s. Améry believed that each land sought the exotic and unusual in the other, not paying attention to whether it was seeing the real face or a caricature.[22] Améry particularly disliked the focus on "unreason" in German culture by French intellectuals such as Michel Foucault.[23] At the same time, Améry noted that stereotypes about French character survived among many Germans, and he feared the decline of French language study in favor of that of English in Germany would contribute to less familiarity with contemporary French culture.[24] Such misunderstandings were not limited to intellectuals. In the early 1980s, one study demonstrated the persistence of stereotypes about national character among schoolchildren in both countries.[25]

Nevertheless, by the 1980s France and Germany were working together to an unprecedented degree. French president François Mitterand could even give a speech in Aachen in 1987 in which he evoked the common Carolingian heritage of France and Germany and their shared destiny.[26] However, the unexpected reunification of East and West Germany in 1989–1990 complicated this cozy relationship and reawakened some old fears in Germany's western neighbor. In his final book, Mitterand gave the impression that he had been in the center of events leading to reunification, when in fact he had been very much on the sidelines and had actually threatened Helmut Kohl's government with the vision of a new Franco-Russian alliance should it not recognize the Oder-Neisse line as Poland's western frontier.[27] In the last resort, however, both France and Germany found themselves having little sway over a process that was largely determined in Moscow and Washington.

Jean-Pierre Chevènement, who had been French minister of labor from 1981 to 1983, expressed many of the fears that the French felt about the newly reunited Germany. These fears were not so much of a resurgence of the old, expansionist *boches*, but rather of an increasing German domination of the European Union and a further erosion of France's ability to pursue an independent course in international politics. Chevènement described a Holy American-German empire of capital, with Germany as a junior partner to the American juggernaut and new world order.[28] Nevertheless, while the fears that Chevènement outlined are very real, they bear little resemblance to those of the old "hereditary enemy." They are based on a rational evaluation of existing trends and do not share in the imaginative constructions of the earlier image of the enemy.

The mythologizing of the enemy in France and Germany was determined to some extent by the conditions of the time. However, the mythologies each side constructed resembled those of other national antagonisms before and since. The transformation of certain qualities possessed by the adversary into negative character traits was a familiar phenomenon of the Cold War. International and interethnic conflict in the Balkans, Africa, and Central Asia has witnessed the revival of old mythologies and the creation of new ones. Many of these struggles seem to occur at crucial points in the development of national and ethnic identity among the participants. When national or ethnic identity is particularly tenuous or faces new challenges it looks outside itself for the inverted mirror and finds comfort in the distorted image presented by the looking glass.

Such enmities are not, however, eternal. The postmodern condition and the decline of the grand narrative in the historical vision of Western nations have made national hatreds seem like atavistic relics of a bygone age. The "hereditary enemies" of a mere generation or two ago are now the peaceful neighbors of today. The experience of two world wars did much to discredit the chauvinistic national imagery of the past. Many French and Germans have even come to think of themselves as "Europeans" first and foremost. This perspective often has its negative aspects, with the right-wing parties in both countries stressing the conservation of "European" identity in the face of immigration from Africa and Asia. However, the identity politics of the present day in both France and Germany is vastly different from what it was a century ago. France and Germany no longer indulge in great power rivalries, choosing instead to pool their resources, and even their currencies, in the European Union. The image of past war no longer raises thoughts of revenge or pride, rather a common revulsion and loathing. No one takes comfort from uncontrollable birth rates, and the revolutions in sexual mores and gender roles have transformed society in both countries. Alsace has ceased to be a question in anybody's mind. And the politics of today in France and Germany has no room for the demonization of erstwhile adversaries become allies. Indeed, the alliance is becoming increasingly important as the United States begins to cut some of its transatlantic ties. Nevertheless, other parts of Europe and much of the rest of the world continue to suffer the consequences of the old mythologies, and new ones may be arising to take their place. One can only hope that recognition of the necessity of addressing the causes of today's national antagonisms and questioning of commonly accepted images will defuse the potential for armed conflict in many parts of the world.

Notes

1. Trans. by Eden and Cedar Paul (New York: Henry Holt and Co., 1933), p. 204. (German original, 1930.)
2. London and New York: Verso, 2001, p. 36.
3. Thomas Raithel, *Das "Wunder" der inneren Einheit: Studien zur deutschen und französischen Öffentlichkeit bei Beginn des Ersten Weltkrieges* (Bonn: Bouvier Verlag, 1996), pp. 342–356, and Troy Paddock, "German Propaganda: The Limits of Gerechtigkeit," in Paddock, ed., *War, Propaganda, and Public Opinion in Newspapers: The Outbreak of the Great War* (Westport, Conn.: Greenwood Press, forthcoming).
4. Hans Weigel, Walter Lukan, and Max D. Peyfuss, *Jeder Schuss ein Russ, jeder Stoss ein Franzos: Literarische und graphische Kriegspropaganda in Deutschland und Österreich 1914–1918* (Vienna: Edition Christian Brandstätter, 1983).
5. Jacques Rivière, *L'Allemand* (Paris: Gallimard, 1918), p. 48.
6. Ibid., p. 54.
7. Karl Lahm, *Franzosen* (Leipzig: Dürr and Weber, 1920), pp. 9–10.
8. André François-Poncet, *De Versailles à Potsdam: la France et le problème allemand contemporain* (Paris: E. Flammarion, 1948), p. 104.
9. For Stresemann's policy toward France, see Michael-Olaf Maxelon, *Stresemann und Frankreich 1914–1929: Deutsche Politik der Ost-West-Balance* (Düsseldorf: Droste Verlag, 1972) and Christian Baechler, *Gustave Stresemann (1878–1929): de l'impérialisme à la sécurité collective* (Strasbourg: Presses universitaires de Strasbourg, 1996).
10. Ernst Schulin, "L'image de la France dans l'opinion de la bourgeoisie allemande (1932–1936)," in Henri Michel et al., *La France et l'Allemagne 1932–1936* (Paris: Editions du Centre National de la Recherche Scientifique, 1980), pp. 94–95.
11. Laird Boswell, "From Liberation to Purge Trials in the 'Mythic Provinces': Recasting French Identities in Alsace and Lorraine, 1918–1920," *French Historical Studies* 23, no. 1 (winter 2000): 129–162.
12. Hermann Alexander Graf Keyserling, *Das Spektrum Europas* (Heidelberg: Niels Kampmann Verlag, 1928), pp. 69–70.
13. *The Civilization of France: An Introduction* (New York: Vintage, 1962; first published 1930), p. 35.
14. Ibid., pp. 221–223.
15. Karl Tögel, *Das wirkliche Frankreich* (Hamburg: Hanseatische Verlagsanstalt, 1934). One wonders how many of the German soldiers at Stalingrad would have preferred a picnic on a summer afternoon.
16. Karl Schwendemann, *Frankreich* (Berlin: Zentral Verlag, 1932), p. 4.
17. Jules Romains, "Que veut l'Allemagne?" *Le couple France-Allemagne* (Paris: E. Flammarion, 1935), pp. 21–22.
18. "Que veut Hitler," ibid., pp. 27–30.
19. Robert d'Harcourt, *Les allemands d'aujourd'hui* (Paris: Librairie Hachette, 1948), pp. 7–14.
20. Ibid., pp. 205–206.
21. Hans-Peter Schwarz, *Erbfreundschaft: Adenauer und Frankreich* (Bonn: Bouvier, 1992), pp. 19–20.
22. Jean Améry, "Deutschland—Frankreich: Misverständnisse und Vorurteile des Geistes," *Neue Rundschau* 87, no. 3 (1976): 441.
23. Ibid., pp. 434–435.
24. Ibid., pp. 437–438.
25. Dieter Tiemann, *Frankreich- und Deutschlandbilder im Widerstreit: Urteile französischer und deutscher Schüler über die Nachbarn am Rhein* (Bonn: Europa Union, 1982).
26. Karl-Heinz Bender, *Mitterand und die deutschen (1938–1995): oder die Wiedervereinigung der Karolinger* (Bonn: Bouvier, 1995), p. 63.
27. François Mitterand, *De l'Allemagne, de la France* (Paris: Editions O. Jacob, 1996).
28. Jean-Pierre Chevènement, *France-Allemagne: parlons franc* (Paris: Plon, 1996), pp. 43–44.

BIBLIOGRAPHY

PRIMARY SOURCES

French

Acker, Paul. *Le soldat Bernard*. Paris: A. Fayard, 1909.

Aderer, Adolphe. *Vers la fin d'une haine*. Paris: Calmann-Lévy, 1907.

Agathon [pseud. of Alexis de Tarde and Henri Massis]. *Les jeunes gens d'aujourd'hui*. Paris: Plon-Nourrit, 1913.

Ajam, Maurice. *Le problème économique franco-allemand*. Paris: Perrin et Cie., 1914.

Albin, Pierre. *La querelle franco-allemande: Le "coup" d'Agadir: origines et développement de la crise de 1911*. Paris: Félix Alcan, 1912.

Andrillon, Bertrand. *L'expansion de l'Allemagne: ses causes, ses formes, ses conséquences*. Paris: M. Riviere et cie., 1914.

Arman, R. d'. *La garde à la frontière: l'armée française en face de l'armée allemande*. Paris: Editions et librairie, 1913.

Arren, Jules. *Guillaume II: ce qu'il dit, ce qu'il pense*. Paris: P. Lafitte et cie., 1911; German trans. *Wilhelm II: Was er sagt, was er denkt*. Leipzig: Historisch-Politischer Verlag, 1911.

Aubert, Georges. *La folie franco-allemande: étude contemporaine*. Paris: E. Flammarion, 1914.

Bainville, Jacques. *L'Allemagne*, vol. 1. Paris: Librairie Plon, 1939.

———. *Le coup d'Agadir et la guerre d'Orient*. Paris: Nouvelle Librairie Nationale, 1913.

Baldy, Robert. *L'Alsace-Lorraine et l'empire allemand (1871–1911)*. Paris, Nancy: Berger-Levrault, 1912.

Barrès, Maurice. *L'œuvre de Maurice Barrès*, vol. 6. Paris: Club de l'Honnête Homme, 1966.

———. *Alsace-Lorraine*. Paris: E. Sansot, 1906.

Baudin, Pierre. *L'empire allemand et l'empereur*. Paris: E. Flammarion, 1911.

Bazin, René. *Les Oberlé*. Paris: Calmann-Lévy, 1901.

Benedetti, Carlos. *Trois ans en Allemagne: usages, moeurs, coutumes, études sociales, administratives et militaires, interviews*. Paris: H. Daragon, 1900.

Bérard, Victor. *La France et Guillaume II*. Paris: A. Colin, 1907 (a series of studies orig. pub. in the *Revue de Paris*).

Berrubé, Emile. *Flottes aériennes en France et en Allemagne: aéroplanes et ballons de guerre*. Paris: Berger-Levrault, 1910.

Blondel, Georges. *Les embarras de l'Allemagne*. Paris: Plon-Nourrit, 1912.

———. *L'essor industriel et commercial du peuple allemand*. 3rd ed. Paris: L. Larose, 1900.

———. *Conférence … sur l'expansion commerciale comparée de la France et de l'Allemagne*. Paris: Librairies-Imprimeries réunies, 1899.

———. *Les transformations sociales de l'Allemagne contemporaine*. Paris: Association ouvrière, 1898.

Bloy, Léon. *Sueur de sang (1870–1871)*. Paris: G. Cres, 1914. Reprinted in *Œuvres complètes*, vol. 6. Paris: Mercure de France, 1967.

Botrel, Théodore. *Coups de clairon: chants et poèmes héroïques*. Paris: G. Ondet, 1903.

Boucher, Arthur. *La France victorieuse dans la guerre de demain*. Rev. ed. Paris: Berger-Levrault, 1912.

Bougle, Célestin. *Les sciences sociales en Allemagne: les méthodes actuelles*. 2nd ed., rev. Paris: F. Alcan, 1902; 3rd ed. 1912.

Bourdon, Georges. *L'enigme allemande: une enquête chez les Allemands*. 3rd ed. Paris: Plon-Nourrit, 1913. Eng. trans. *The German Enigma: Being an Inquiry Among the Germans as to What They Think, What They Want, What They Can Do.* Trans. by Beatrice Marshall. London: J. M. Dent and Sons, 1914.

Bruneau, Louis. *L'Allemagne en France: enquêtes économiques*. Paris: Plon-Nourrit, 1914.

Brunet, Réné. *La nationalité dans l'empire allemand*. Paris: Giard, 1912.

Bruno, G [pseud. of Mme. Alfred Fouillée]. *Le tour de la France par deux enfants*. Paris: Librairie Classique Eugène Belin, 1877.

Cahu, Théodore, and Louis Forest. *L'oubli?* Published as a supplement to *L'Illustration*, 29 July 1899–4 November 1899.

Cambon, Victor. *Les derniers progrès de l'Allemagne*. 3rd ed. Paris: P. Roger, 1914.

———. *L'Allemagne au travail*. Paris: P. Roger, 1910.

Celarié, Henriette. *Au pair: une Française en Allemagne*. Paris: Armand Colin, 1911.

Champsaur, Félicien. *L'abattoir (1870–1871)*. Paris: L'Ermitage, 1910.

Chéradame, André. *La crise française*. 3rd ed. Paris: Plon-Nourrit, 1912.

———. *Le monde et la guerre russo-japonaise*. Paris: Plon-Nourrit et Cie., 1906.

———. *La colonisation et les colonies allemandes*. Paris: Plon-Nourrit, 1905.

———. *L'Affaire Dreyfus à l'étranger*. Paris: F. Levé, 1899.

Civrieux, Commandant de. *Le germanisme encerclé*. Paris: H. Charles-Lavauzelle, 1913.

Combes, Paul. *La guerre possible*. Paris: Librairie illustrée, 1906.

Danrit, Capitaine. *Alert!* Paris: Flammarion, 1914.

Daudet, Léon. *L'avant-guerre: études et documents sur l'espionnage juif-allemand en France depuis l'affaire Dreyfus*. Paris: Nouvelle librairie nationale, 1913.

Dejean, Georges. *La menace allemande*. Grenoble: Imprimerie générale, 1914. German trans. *Die deutsche Drohung*. Oldenburg: Gerhard Stalling, 1914.

Delahache, Georges [pseud. of Lucien Aaron]. *Alsace-Lorraine: la carte au liséré vert*. 4th ed. Paris: Hachette, 1911.

Delaisi, Francis. *La guerre qui vient*. Paris: Edition de la "Guerre Sociale," 1911. Eng. trans. *The Inevitable War*. Boston: Small, Maynard and Co., 1915.

———. *La force allemande*. Paris: Librairie de Pages libres, 1905.

Denis, Ernest. *La fondation de l'empire allemand, 1852–1871*. Paris: A. Colin, 1906.

Déroulede, Paul. *1870: feuilles de route.* Paris: Librairie Félix Juven, 1907.

———. *Chants du soldat: marches et sonneries.* Paris: Calmann-Lévy, 1884.

Ducrocq, Georges. *Les provinces inébranlables: l'Austrasie, la question d'Alsace-Lorraine, Metz, la Wallonie.* Paris: Les Marches de l'Est, 1913.

———. *La blessure mal fermée: notes d'un voyageur en Alsace-Lorraine.* Paris: Plon-Nourrit, 1910.

Dupouy, Auguste. *France et Allemagne, littératures comparées.* Paris: P. Delaplane, 1913.

Dupuis, Victor César Eugene. *L'évolution militaire en Allemagne et en France: Essais de sociologie militaire.* Paris: G. Kleiner, 1901.

Esparbes, Georges d'. *L'épopée française.* Paris: C. Delagrave, 1910.

Espé de Metz, G. *70, Cinq tableaux de la guerre.* Paris: L. Fournier, 1911.

Estournelles de Constant, Paul Henri Benjamin, baron d'. *En Allemagne: le remède à la paix armée.* Paris: C. Delagrave, 1910.

———. *La politique extérieure de la France: le respect des autres races.* Paris: C. Delagrave, 1910.

Félix, Pierre. *Après le traité franco-allemand et maintenant?... le désarmament ou la guerre!* Paris: B. Grasset, 1912.

Fouillée, Alfred. *Esquisse psychologique des peuples européens.* Paris: Félix Alcan, 1903; 5th ed. 1914.

François-Poncet, André. *Ce que pense la jeunesse allemande.* Paris: G. Oudin, 1913.

Gaston, Henry. *Où va l'Allemagne: A la faillite? A la guerre? A la révolution?* Paris: Editions et librairie, 1913.

Gerber, Philippe. *La condition de l'Alsace-Lorraine dans l'Empire Allemand.* Lille: H. Morel, 1906.

Gobat, Albert. *La Conférence interparlementaire franco-allemande de Berne.* Bern: G. Grunau, 1913.

———. *Le cauchemar de l'Europe.* Strasbourg and Paris: Treuttel and Wurtz; Le Soudier, 1911.

Goyau, Georges. *Jeanne d'Arc devant l'opinion allemande.* Paris: Perrin et Cie., 1907.

———. *Vieille France, jeune Allemagne* (Paris: Perrin et Cie., 1904).

Grand-Carteret, John. *France—Allemagne—Maroc: une victoire sans guerre.* Paris: Schleicher, 1911 (a German translation appeared the same year).

———. *Le rapprochement franco-allemand par l'amélioration du sort de l'Alsace-Lorraine.* Bonn: A. Ahn, 1911.

———. *Derrière "Lui": l'homosexualité en Allemagne.* Paris: E. Bernard, 1908. Repr. ed. Paris: Gai-Kitsch-Camp, 1992.

———. *Images galantes et esprit de l'etranger: Berlin, Munich, Vienne, Turin, Londres.* Paris: La Librairie mondiale, 1907.

———. *"Lui" devant l'objectif caricatural.* 2nd ed. Paris: Nilsson, 1906 (a German translation appeared the same year).

Gravereaux, L. *Les discussions sur le patriotisme et le militarisme dans les congrès socialistes.* Paris: G. Dussardier & P. Frank, 1913.

Grouard, Auguste Antoine. *France et Allemagne: la guerre éventuelle.* 4th ed. Paris: Chapelot, 1913.

Guieysse, Charles. *La France et la paix armée: la Conférence de La Haye.* Paris: Librairie de "Pages libres," 1905.

Guilland, Antoine. *L'Allemagne nouvelle et ses historiens.* Paris: F. Alcan, 1899.

Hallays, André. *A travers l'Alsace.* Paris: Perrin et Cie., 1911.

Hansi (pseud. of Jean-Jacques Waltz). *Mon village, ceux qui n'oublient pas.* Paris: H. Floury, 1914.

———. *L'histoire d'Alsace: racontée aux petits enfants d'Alsace et de France.* Paris: H. Floury, 1913.

———. *Professor Knatschké: œuvres choisies du Grand Savant Allemand et de sa fille Elsa.* Paris: H. Floury, 1912.

Hayem, Emile. *Menace prussienne: la riposte* ... Paris: H. Charles-Lavauzelle, 1911.

Heimweh, Jean (pseud. of Fernand de Dartein). *Allemagne, France, Alsace-Lorraine.* Paris: Armand Colin, 1899.

Hervé, Gustave. *L'Alsace-Lorraine.* Paris: Editions de la "Guerre Sociale," 1913; German trans. Munich, 1913.

———. *Histoire de la France pour les grands.* Paris: Bibliotheque d'éducation, 1910.

———. *Le Congrès de Stuttgart et l'antipatriotisme.* Paris: Editions de la "Guerre Sociale,"1907.

Hinzelin, Emile. *L'Alsace sous le joug.* Paris: Editions et librairie, 1914.

———. *Coeurs d'Alsace et de Lorraine.* 3rd ed. Paris: Librairie Delagrave, 1913.

———. *En Alsace-Lorraine.* Paris: Plon-Nourrit, 1904.

Hoche, Jules. *L'empereur Guillaume II intime.* Paris: Librairie Félix Juven, 1906.

Hubert, Lucien. *L'effort allemand: l'Allemagne et la France au point de vue économique.* Paris: F. Alcan, 1911.

Huret, Jules. *L'Allemagne moderne* (Paris: P. Lafitte, 1913).

———. *En Allemagne: La Bavière et la Saxe.* Paris: E. Fasquelle, 1911.

———. *En Allemagne: Berlin.* Paris: E. Fasquelle, 1909.

———. *En Allemagne: De Hambourg aux marches de Pologne.* Paris: E. Fasquelle, 1908.

———. *En Allemagne: Rhin et Westphalie.* Paris: E. Fasquelle, 1907.

Is, Jean d' (pseud. of Miche de Malleray, Henri Charles Joseph). *Impressions d'un soldat: A travers l'Allemagne.* Paris: Plon-Nourrit, 1914; new ed. 1916.

Ivoi, Paul d', and Colonel Royet. *La patrie en danger: histoire de la guerre future.* Paris: Geoffroy, 1905.

Jacques, Hubert. *L'Allemagne et la Légion.* Paris: Chapelot, 1914.

Jaurès, Jean. *Œuvres.* 9 vols., Paris: Rieder, 1931–1939.

Jousset, Paul. *L'Allemagne contemporaine illustrée.* Paris: Larousse, 1902.

Lair, Maurice. *L'impérialisme allemand.* 3rd ed. Paris: A. Colin, 1914.

Lanoir, Paul. *L'espionnage allemand en France: son organisation, ses dangers, les remèdes nécessaires.* Paris: Cocuaud et cie., 1908. Eng. trans. *The German Spy System in France.* London: Mills and Boon, n.d.

Laurent, Marcel. *La paix armée et le problème d'Alsace dans l'opinion des nouvelles générations françaises.* Paris: n.p., 1914.

Lavaur, J.-H. *La fin de l'empire allemand pour 1913: d'après plusieurs prophéties célèbres, précises et concordantes (Prophéties d'Hermann; prophéties de Mayence; prédictions de Fiensberg).* Paris: Editions pratiques et documentaires, 1913.

Lavisse, Ernest. *Histoire de France: cours élémentaire.* Paris: Armand Colin, 1913.

Le Bas, Georges. *Le roman allemand.* Paris: Louis-Michaud, 1910.

Leblond, Marius. *La France devant l'Europe* ... Paris: E. Fasquelle, 1913.

Legendre, Maurice. *La guerre prochaine et la mission de la France.* Paris: Marcel Riviere, 1913.

Leroy, Maxime. *L'Alsace-Lorraine: porte de France, porte d'Allemagne* ... Paris: P. Ollendorff, 1914.

Lichtenberger, André. *Juste Lobel, Alsacien.* Paris: Plon, 1911.

Lichtenberger, Henri. *L'Allemagne moderne: son évolution*. Paris: Flammarion, 1912. Eng. trans. *Germany and its Evolution in Modern Times*. Trans. by Anthony Mario Ludovici; New York: H. Holt, 1913.

Longuet, Jean. *Les socialistes allemands contre la guerre et le militarisme*. Paris, 1913.

Louis, Désiré. *Souvenirs d'un prisonnier de guerre en Allemagne (1870–1871)*. Paris: F. Juven, 1899.

Margueritte, Victor. *Les frontières du coeur*. Paris: Flammarion, 1912.

Margueritte, Paul and Victor. *Histoire de la guerre de 1870–71*. Paris: Hachette, 1912.

———. *Le désastre*. Paris: Plon-Nourrit, 1898.

Martin, William. *La crise politique de l'Allemagne contemporaine*. Paris: Félix Alcan, 1913.

Martin du Gard, Roger. *Jean Barois*. Paris: Editions de la Nouvelle revue française, 1913.

Maurras, Charles. *Kiel et Tanger, 1895–1905: la République française devant l'Europe*. Paris: Nouvelle librairie nationale, 1910.

Mazé, Jules. *L'année terrible: la défense de Paris: armées du nord, des Vosges et de l'est*. Tours: A. Mame, 1909.

Méténier, Oscar. *Les Berlinois chez eux: vertus et vices allemands*. Paris: Albin Michel, n.d. (1908).

Mévil, André. *De la paix de Francfort à la Conférence d'Algésiras*. Paris: Plon-Nourrit, 1909.

———. *La paix est malade*. Paris: Plon, 1914.

Milhaud, Edgard. *La démocratie socialiste allemande*. Paris: Félix Alcan, 1903.

Moysset, Henri. *L'esprit publique en Allemagne vingt ans après Bismarck*. Paris: Félix Alcan, 1911.

Normand, R. *Le patriotisme allemand: ses origines, son évolution, les débuts du pangermanisme*. Paris: L. Fournier, 1910.

Noussanne, Henri de. *Le véritable Guillaume II*. Paris: Société d'éditions et de publications, 1904.

Novicow, J. *L'Alsace-Lorraine: obstacle à l'expansion allemande*. Paris: Felix Alcan, 1913.

Palat, Général [pseud. of Pierre Lehautcourt]. *L'alliance franco-allemande ou la guerre*. Paris: Librairie Chapelot, 1914.

Péguy, Charles. "Note conjointe sur M. Descartes et la philosophie cartésienne" (1914). In *Œuvres en prose, 1909–1914*. Paris: Gallimard, 1959.

Pevet, Alfred. *L'Allemagne contemporaine*. Paris: La Fidélité, 1914.

———. *Raisons historiques et actuelles d'un rapprochement franco-allemand*. Paris: Imprimerie de l'Emancipatrice, 1913.

Phélip, Gaston. *Voix d'Alsace et de Lorraine*. Paris: Editions et librairie, 1911.

Pilant, Paul. *Le péril allemand*. Paris: Editions et librairie, 1913.

———. *Le patriotisme en France et à l'étranger*. Paris: Perrin et Cie., 1912.

Pinon, René. *France et Allemagne 1870–1913*. Paris: Libraires-Editeurs, 1913.

Prévost, Marcel. *Monsieur et Madame Moloch*. Paris: A. Fayard, 1906.

Psichari, Ernest. *L'appel des armes*. Paris: G. Oudin et cie., 1910. Reprinted in *Œuvres complètes*. Paris: L. Conrad, 1948.

Raynaud, Ernest. *Les deux Allemagnes: poèmes*. Paris: Mercure de France, 1914.

Régamey, Jeanne. *Jeune Alsace: roman*. Paris: Nouvelle librairie nationale, 1909.

Régamey, Jeanne and Frederic. *L'Allemagne ennemie*. Paris: Albin Michel, 1913.

Renan, Ernest. *Œuvres complètes*, vol. 1. Paris: Calmann-Lévy, 1947.

Rey, Etienne. *La renaissance de l'orgueil français*. Paris: B. Grasset, 1912.

Reynaud, Louis. *Histoire générale de l'influence française en Allemagne*. Reprint ed. New York: Lenox Hill, 1971. Orig. pub. 1914.

Rivière, Jacques. *L'Allemand*. Paris: Gallimard, 1918.

Roche, Jules. *Allemagne et France*. Paris: E. Flammarion, 1898.

Rolland, Romain. *Jean Christophe*. Paris: Ollendorff, 1910–1929.

Romains, Jules. *Le couple France-Allemagne*. Paris: E. Flammarion, 1935.

Sembat, Marcel. *Faites un roi, sinon faites la paix*. 12th ed. Paris: E. Figuiere, 1913.

Serrigny, Bernard. *L'évolution de l'empire allemand: de 1871 jusqu'à nos jours*. Paris: Perrin et Cie., 1914.

Tardieu, André. *Le mystére d'Agadir*. Paris: Calmann-Levy, 1912.

——. *Le prince de Bulow: l'homme et le milieu, la politique extérieure, la politique intérieure*. Paris: Calmann-Levy, 1909. German trans. 1910.

——. *La Conférence d'Algesiras: histoire diplomatique de la crise marocaine (15 janvier–7 avril 1906)*. 2nd ed. Paris: F. Alcan, 1908.

——. *France and the Alliances: The Struggle for the Balance of Power*. New York: The MacMillan Co., 1908.

Tournier, Gaston. *A travers l'Allemagne religieuse: Impressions et souvenirs*. Paris: Fischbacher, 1912.

Valéry, Paul. "Une conquête méthodique." In *Œuvres*, vol. 1. Paris: Gallimard, 1957.

Vergnet, Paul. *La France en danger: l'œuvre des pangermanistes, ce qu'il sont, ce qu'ils peuvent, ce qu'ils veulent*. Paris: La Renaissance du livre, 1913.

Vogüé, Eugène-Melchior, vicomte de. "Impressions d'Allemagne." In *Pages d'histoire*. Paris: Armand Colin, 1902.

Weindel, Henri de and F.-P. Fischer. *L'homosexualité en Allemagne: étude documentaire et anecdotique*. Paris: F. Juven, 1908.

Welschinger, Henri. *La guerre de 1870: causes et responsabilités*. Paris: Plon-Nourrit, 1910.

——. *Bismarck*. Paris: Félix Alcan, 1900.

Zola, Emile et al. *Les Soirées de Médan*. Paris: Fasquelle, 1955.

Zola, Emile. *La débâcle*. Paris: Bibliothèque Charpentier, 1892.

Newspapers and Journals

L'Assiette au Beurre
L'Aurore
Le Figaro
Le Matin
Le Petit Journal
Le Petit Parisien
La Revue Bleue
La Revue des Deux Mondes
Le Temps

German

(Anon.) *Im Kampf um die Kunst: die Antwort auf den "Protest deutscher Künstler."* Munich: R. Piper, 1911.

(Anon.) *Das Staatsverbrechen des Generals Boisdeffre: Ein Beitrag zur Aufklärung der Dreyfusangelegenheit.* Berlin: Hermann Walther, 1899.

(Anon.) *Unser Kaiser und sein Volk! Deutsche Sorgen: Von einem Schwarzseher.* Freiburg i. B., Leipzig: P. Waetzel, 1906. French trans. 1907.

Arndt, Paul. *Grundzüge der auswärtigen Politik Deutschlands.* Jena: E. Diederichs, 1912.

Baedeker, Karl. *Paris and Environs.* Leipzig: K. Baedeker, 1913.

———. *Northern France.* Leipzig: K. Baedeker, 1909.

Bernhardi, Friedrich von. *Deutschland und der nächste Krieg.* Stuttgart and Berlin: J. G. Cotta, 1912. Eng. trans. *Germany and the Next War.* Trans. by Allen H. Powles; New York: C. A. Eron, 1914.

———. *Unsere Zukunft: Ein Mahnwort an das deutsche Volk.* Stuttgart and Berlin: J.G. Cotta, 1912.

Beyerlein, Franz Adam. *Jena oder Sedan.* Berlin: Vita, 1903. Eng. trans. *Jena or Sedan.* London: William Heinemann, 1914.

Bleibtreu, Karl. *Belfort: die Kämpfe von Dijon bis Pontarlier.* 3rd ed. Stuttgart: Carl Krabbe, 1911.

———. *Strassburg: Ein Tagebuch der Belagerung.* Stuttgart: Carl Krabbe, 1910.

———. *Beaumont.* Stuttgart: Carl Krabbe, 1909.

———. *Le Mans.* Stuttgart: Carl Krabbe, 1909.

———. *Orleans.* Stuttgart: Carl Krabbe, 1909.

———. *Weissenburg.* Stuttgart: Carl Krabbe, 1909.

———. *Woerth.* 3rd ed. Stuttgart: Carl Krabbe, 1909.

———. *St. Privat.* Stuttgart: Carl Krabbe, 1908.

———. *Der Verrat von Metz.* Stuttgart: Carl Krabbe, 1908.

———. *Die Kommune.* Stuttgart: Carl Krabbe, 1905.

———. *Colombey.* Stuttgart: Carl Krabbe, 1904.

———. *Dies Irae: Erinnerungen eines französischen Offiziers an Sedan.* 5th ed. Stuttgart: Carl Krabbe, 1904.

———. *Amiens–St. Quentin.* 2nd ed. Stuttgart: Carl Krabbe, 1903.

———. *Spicheren.* Stuttgart: Carl Krabbe, 1903.

———. *Die Wahrheit über 1870.* Munich: Deutsch-französische Rundschau, 1901.

———. *Gravelotte: die Kämpfe um Metz.* 2nd ed. Stuttgart: Carl Krabbe, 1899.

———. *Paris, 1870–1871.* 2nd ed. Stuttgart: Carl Krabbe, 1899.

———. *Sedan.* Stuttgart: Gussman, n.d.

Bloem, Walter. (1) *Das eiserne Jahr.* Leipzig: Grethlein, 1910.

———. (3) *Die Schmiede der Zukunft.* Leipzig: Grethlein, 1913.

———. *Das verlorene Vaterland.* Leipzig: Grethlein, 1911.

———. (2) *Volk wider Volk.* Leipzig: Grethlein, 1912.

Bülow, Bernhard, Fürst von. *Imperial Germany.* London: Cassell and Co., 1914.

Cartellieri, Alexander. *Deutschland und Frankreich im Wandel der Jahrhunderte.* Jena: G. Fischer, 1914.

Claß, Heinrich. *Wenn ich der Kaiser wär': Politische Wahrheiten und Notwendigkeiten.* Leipzig: Dieterich, 1913.

Curtius, Ernst Robert. *The Civilization of France: An Introduction.* New York: Vintage, 1962. First published 1930.

————. *Maurice Barrès und die geistigen Grundlagen des französischen Nationalismus.* Hildesheim: Georg Olms, 1962. First published 1921.

Distelbarth, Paul. *Lebendiges Frankreich.* Berlin: Rowohlt Verlag, 1936.

————. *Neues Werden in Frankreich: Zeugnisse führender Franzosen.* Stuttgart: Ernst Klett, 1938.

Engel, Eduard. *Geschichte der französischen Literatur.* 8th ed. Leipzig: F. Brand-Stetter, 1912.

————. *Psychologie der französischen Literatur.* 3rd ed. Berlin: L. Simion, 1904.

Ermels, Robert. *Frankreichs Koloniale Handelspolitik: Geschichte, Wirkung und Kritik derselben.* Berlin: R. Trenkel, 1910.

Estournelles de Constant, Paul Henri Benjamin, baron d'. *Frankreich und Deutschland.* Berlin: W. Kohlhammer, 1913.

————. *Die französisch-deutsche Annäherung als Grundlage des Weltfriedens.* Berlin: Simion, 1909.

Feiler, Arthur. *Die Konjunktur-Periode 1907–1913 in Deutschland.* Jena: G. Fischer, 1914.

Fernau, Hermann. *Die französische Demokratie: Sozialpolitische Studien aus Frankreichs Kulturwerkstatt.* Munich: Duncker & Humblot, 1914.

Flake, Otto. *Rund um die elsässische Frage.* Karlsruhe: Dreililien Verlag, 1911.

Friedmann, Fritz. *Deutschland—Frankreich und Kaiser Wilhelm II: Eine Völkerstudie.* Berlin: A. Pulvermacher & Co., 1912.

Gaedke, R. *Krieg oder Frieden? Unsere Aussichten in einem künftigen Krieg.* Berlin: n.p., 1907.

Gans, Kurt. *Unser Verhältnis zu England und Frankreich.* Wiesbaden: K. Schwab, 1911.

Geißler, Max. *Valentin Upp, der Legionär: Nach Berichten eines alten Afrikaners.* Leipzig: Otto Spamer, 1914.

Gensel, Walther. *Paris: Studien und Eindrücke.* Leipzig: Theodor Weicher, 1900.

Haas, Joseph. *Frankreich, Land und Staat.* Heidelberg: C. Winter, 1910.

Hepke, Felix Victor von. *Frankreich: Das Heer am Ende des neunzehnten Jahrhunderts.* Berlin: Schall, 1900.

Hildebrand, Gerhard. *Sozialistische Auslandspolitik: Betrachtungen über die weltpolitische Lage anlässlich des Marokko-Streites.* Jena: E. Diederichs, 1911. French trans., 1912.

Hillebrand, Karl. *Frankreich und die Franzosen.* 4th ed. Strassburg: K.J. Trübner, 1898. Arno Reprint ed., 1979. Eng. trans. *France and the French.* New York: Scribner and Welford, 1881.

Hocker, Gustav. *1870 und 1871: Zwei Jahre deutschen Heldenthums* (Glogau: C. Flemming, 1906).

Höcker, Oskar. *Der Nationalkrieg gegen Frankreich in den Jahren 1870 und 1871: Ehrentage aus Deutschlands neuester Geschichte.* 8th ed. Leipzig: O. Spamer, 1900.

Hopf, Julius, and Karl Paulsiek, eds. *Deutsches Lesebuch für höhere Lehranstalten.* Berlin: Mittler, 1907.

Hummel, Anton. *Bis Algier und Lourdes: Eine Reise durch Frankreich.* 2nd ed. Ravensburg: Verlag der Dorn'schen Buchhandlung, 1899.

Kautsky, Karl. *Patriotismus und Sozialdemokratie.* Leipzig: Buchdruckerei Aktiengesellschaft, 1907.

Klemperer, Victor. *Curriculum Vitae: Jugend um 1900.* Berlin: Siedler Verlag, 1989.

Kohut, Adolph. *Frankreich als Erbfeind Deutschlands.* Hof a. S.: H. Kleemeier, 1914.

Lahm, Karl. *Franzosen.* Leipzig: Dürr and Weber, 1920.

Lamszus, Wilhelm. *Das Menschenschlachthaus: Bilder vom kommenden Krieg.* Hamburg: A. Janssen, 1912.

Liliencron, Detlev von. *Kriegsnovellen.* In *Gesammelte Werke,* vol. 7. Berlin: Schuster and Loeffler, 1912.

Lepsius, Johannes, Albrecht Mendelssohn-Bartholdy, and Friedrich Thimme, eds. *Die große Politik der europäischen Kabinette, 1871–1914: Sammlung der diplomatischen Akten des Auswärtigen Amtes.* Berlin: Deutsche Verlagsgesellschaft für Politik und Geschichte, 1922–1927.

Mann-Tiechler, K. H. von. *Deutschland und Frankreich: politische und militärische Betrachtungen am Anfang des zwanzigsten Jahrhunderts.* Berlin: F. Luckhardt, 1903.

Martin, Rudolf. *Stehen wir vor einem Weltkrieg?* Leipzig: Friedrich Engelmann, 1908.

Naumann, Friedrich. *Werke.* Vol. 6, *Ästhetische Schriften.* Cologne: Westdeutscher Verlag, 1964.

Nippold, Otfried. *Der deutsche Chauvinismus.* Berlin: W. Kohlhammer, 1913. 2nd ed. Bern, 1917.

———. *Die auswärtige Politik und die öffentliche Meinung.* Berlin: W. Kohlhammer, 1913.

Nossig, Alfred. *Die Politik des Weltfriedens: Die deutsch-französische Annäherung und die Kontinentalunion.* Berlin: Hermann Walther, 1900.

Osten-Sacken und von Rhein, Ottomar, Frhr. v.d. *Deutschlands nächster Krieg.* Berlin: Bath, 1905.

Pflugk-Harttung, Julius von. *The Franco-German War, 1870–1871.* London: S. Sonnenschein, 1900.

Plehn, Hans. *Deutsche Weltpolitik und kein Krieg.* Berlin: Puttkammer und Muhlbrecht, 1913.

Regensberg, Friedrich. *1870/71: Der deutsch-französische Krieg.* Stuttgart: Franckh, 1907.

Rehtwisch, Theodor. *Die grosse Zeit: ein Jahrhundertbuch.* Leipzig: G. Wigand, 1913.

Riezler, Kurt (under the pseud. J. J. Ruedorffer). *Grundzüge der Weltpolitik in der Gegenwart.* Stuttgart: Deutsche Verlagsanstalt, 1914.

———. *Die Erforderlichkeit des Unmöglichen.* Munich: G. Muller, 1913.

Rohrbach, Paul. *Der deutsche Gedanke in der Welt.* Konigstein im Taunus: K. R. Langewiesche, 1914.

———. *Deutschland unter den Weltvölkern: Materialien zur auswärtigen Politik.* Berlin-Schoneberg: Buchverlag der "Hilfe," 1911. 3rd ed. 1912.

Rosen, Erwin. *In der Fremdenlegion: Erinnerungen und Eindrücke.* 8th ed. Stuttgart: R. Lutz, 1914.

Rossmann, Philipp. *Ein Studienaufenthalt in Paris: Ein Führer für Studierende, Lehrer und Lehrerinnen.* Marburg: N. G. Elwert, 1900.

Rühlmann, Paul. *Der Staatsbürgerliche Unterricht in Frankreich (instruction morale et civique).* Leipzig, Berlin: B. G. Teubner, 1912.

Schäfer, Dietrich. *Deutschland und Frankreich.* Berlin: Kameradschaft, 1914.

Schiemann, Theodor. *Deutschland und die Grosse Politik.* Berlin: G. Reimer, 1901–1914. (Collection of weekly reviews from *Neue Preußische Zeitung.*)

Schirmacher, Kathe. *Deutschland und Frankreich seit 35 Jahren: Ein Beitrag zur Kulturgeschichte.* Berlin: Bard Marquardt & Co., 1906.

Schmitz, Oscar A. H. *Was uns Frankreich war*. 7th ed. Munich: Georg Müller, 1914. Originally titled *Das Land der Wirklichkeit: die französischen Gesellschaftsprobleme*.

Schwendemann, Karl. *Frankreich*. Berlin: Zentral-Verlag, 1932.

Sieburg, Friedrich. *Gott in Frankreich? Ein Versuch*. Frankfurt a. M.: Societäts-Verlag, 1932.

Sombart, Werner. *The Quintessence of Capitalism: A Study of the History and Psychology of the Modern Business Man*. Trans. by M. Epstein; New York: Howard Fertig, 1967.

Sommerfeld, Adolf. *Frankreichs Ende im Jahre 19??: Ein Zukunftsbild*. Berlin: Verlag Continent, 1912.

Stählin, Karl. *Der Deutsch-Französische Krieg 1870/71*. Heidelberg: K. Winters Universitäts Buchhandlung, 1912.

Teubner, L. *Eine Woche in Paris*. Berlin: Georg Stilke, 1909.

Tögel, Karl. *Das wirkliche Frankreich*. Hamburg: Hanseatische Verlagsanstalt, 1934.

Uhde, Wilhelm. *Paris: Eine Impression*. Berlin: Bard, Marquardt, 1904.

Villatte, Césaire. *Land und Leute in Frankreich*. Berlin: Langenscheidtsche Verlagsbuchhandlung, 1904.

Vinnen, Carl. *Ein Protest deutscher Künstler*. Jena: Diederich, 1911.

Wahl, Adalbert. "Das zeitgenössische Frankreich." In *Handbuch der Politik*. Vol. 2, *Die Aufgaben der Politik*. Berlin and Leipzig: W. Rothschild, 1912–1913.

Wechssler, Eduard. *Die Franzosen und wir: Der Wandel in der Schätzung deutscher Eigenart 1871–1914*. Jena: Diederichs, 1915.

Wershoven, F. J. (Franz Josef). *Frankreich: Lese-und Realienbuch für den französischen Unterricht*. 5th ed. Cothen: O. Schulze, 1910.

Wieland, Ernest. *Welscher Witz: ein Franzosenspiegel in Anekdoten aus dem 16. bis 19. Jahrhundert*. Stuttgart: Strecker & Schroder, 1914.

Wolff, Theodor. *Pariser Tagebuch*. Munich: Albert Langen, 1908.

Woltmann, Ludwig. *Die Germanen in Frankreich: Eine Untersuchung über den Einfluss der germanischen Rasse auf die Geschichte und Kultur Frankreichs*. Jena: E. Diederichs, 1907.

Zweig, Stefan. *The World of Yesterday*. New York: Viking Press, 1943.

Newspapers and Journals

Berliner Tageblatt
Deutsche Revue
Frankfurter Zeitung
Kölnische Zeitung
Münchner Neueste Nachrichten
Neue Preußische Zeitung
Die Neue Zeit
Norddeutsche Allgemeine Zeitung
Simplicissimus
Sozialistische Monatshefte
Vossische Zeitung
Die Zukunft

SECONDARY SOURCES

Abret, Helga, and Michel Grunewald, eds. *Visions allemandes de la France, 1871–1914*. Bern, New York: P. Lang, 1995.

Afflerbach, Holger. *Falkenhayn: Politisches Denken und Handeln im Kaiserreich*. Munich: R. Oldenbourg, 1996.

Agulhon, Maurice. *Marianne au pouvoir: l'imagerie et la symbolique républicaines de 1880 à 1914*. Paris: E. Flammarion, 1989.

Aho, James A. *This Thing of Darkness: A Sociology of the Enemy*. Seattle: University of Washington Press, 1994.

Allain, Jean Claude. *Agadir 1911: une crise impérialiste en Europe pour la conquête du Maroc*. Paris: Université de Paris I, 1976.

Améry, Jean. "Deutschland—Frankreich: Misverständnisse und Vorurteile des Geistes." *Neue Rundschau* 87, no. 3 (1976): 429–444.

Anderson, Eugene N. *The First Moroccan Crisis 1904–1906*. Hamden, Conn.: Archon Books, 1966. First published 1930.

Andler, Charles. *Vie de Lucien Herr*. Paris: Rieder, 1932.

———. *Le socialisme impérialiste dans l'Allemagne contemporaine: dossier d'une polémique avec Jean Jaurès (1912–1913)*. Brussels: Bossard, 1918.

———. *Le pangermanisme colonial sous Guillaume II*. Paris: L. Conard, 1916.

———. *Le pangermanisme contintental sous Guillaume II*. Paris: L. Conard, 1915.

Andrew, Christopher. *Théophile Delcassé and the Making of the Entente Cordiale: A Reappraisal of French Foreign Policy 1898–1905*. New York: St. Martin's Press, 1968.

Baechler, Christian. *Gustave Stresemann (1878–1929): de l'impérialisme à la sécurité collective*. Strasbourg: Presses universitaires de Strasbourg, 1996.

Barbey-Say, Hélène. *Le voyage de France en Allemagne de 1871 à 1914: voyages et voyageurs français dans l'empire germanique*. Nancy: Presses universitaires de Nancy, 1994.

Barcelo, Laurent. *Paul d'Estournelles de Constant: l'expression d'une idée européenne*. Paris: Editions L'Harmattan, 1995.

Bariéty, Jacques, et al. *La France et l'Allemagne entre les deux guerres mondiales: actes du colloque tenu en Sorbonne (Paris IV), 15–16–17 janvier 1987*. Nancy: Presses universitaires de Nancy, 1987.

Barraclough, Geoffrey. *From Agadir to Armageddon: Anatomy of a Crisis*. New York: Holmes and Meier, 1982.

Barral, Pierre. "L'Alsace-Lorraine: trois départements sous la botte." In Jean-Pierre Azéma and François Bédarida, eds., *La France des années noires*. Vol. 1, *De la défaite à Vichy*. Paris: Editions du Seuil, 1993.

Becker, Jean-Jacques. *1914: Comment les français sont entrés dans la guerre*. Paris: Presses de la Fondation nationale des sciences politiques, 1977.

———. *Le Carnet B: les pouvoirs publics et l'antimilitarisme avant la guerre de 1914*. Paris: Editions Klincksieck, 1973.

Bellanger, Claude, ed. *Histoire générale de la presse française*. Paris: Presses universitaires de France, 1976.

Bender, Karl-Heinz. *Mitterrand und die Deutschen (1938–1995): oder die Wiedervereinigung der Karolinger*. Bonn: Bouvier, 1995.

Berg, Manfred. *Gustav Stresemann: Eine politische Karriere zwischen Reich und Republik*. Göttingen: Muster-Schmidt Verlag, 1992.

Binion, Rudolph. *Defeated Leaders: The Political Fate of Caillaux, Jouvenel, and Tardieu.* New York: Columbia University Press, 1960.

Binoche, Jacques. *Histoire des relations franco-allemandes de 1789 à nos jours.* Paris: A. Colin, 1996.

———. *De Gaulle et les Allemands.* Bruxelles: Complexe, 1990.

Boemeke, Manfred F., Roger Chickering, and Stig Förster, eds. *Anticipating Total War: The German and American Experiences, 1871–1914.* Cambridge: Cambridge University Press, 1999.

Bolle, Fritz. "Darwinismus und Zeitgeist. " In H. J. Schoeps, ed., *Das Wilhelminische Zeitalter.* Stuttgart: E. Klett, 1967.

Boswell, Laird. "From Liberation to Purge Trials in the 'Mythic Provinces': Recasting French Identities in Alsace and Lorraine, 1918–1920." *French Historical Studies* 23, no. 1 (2000): 129–162.

Boulding, Kenneth E. *The Image.* Ann Arbor: University of Michigan Press, 1956.

———. "National Images and International Systems." *Journal of Conflict Resolution* 3, no. 2 (1959): 120–131.

Bredin, Jean-Denis. *Joseph Caillaux.* Paris: Hachette, 1985.

Brummert, Ulrike. *Jean Jaurès: Frankreich, Deutschland und die Zweite Internationale am Vorabend des Ersten Weltkrieges.* Tübingen: G. Narr, 1989.

Burac, Robert. *Charles Péguy: la révolution et la grace.* Paris: R. Laffont, 1994.

Burgelin, Henri. "Le mythe de l'ennemi héréditaire dans les relations franco-allemandes." *Documents: Revue des questions allemandes* (1979): 76–88.

Burrin, Philippe. *Living with Defeat: France under the German Occupation 1940–1944.* Trans. by Janet Lloyd. London: Arnold, 1996.

Caron, Vicki. *Between France and Germany: The Jews of Alsace-Lorraine 1871–1918.* Stanford: Stanford University Press, 1988.

Carré, Jean Marie. *Les écrivains français et le mirage allemand, 1800–1940.* Paris: Boivin, 1947.

Carroll, E. Malcolm. *Germany and the Great Powers 1866–1914: A Study in Public Opinion and Foreign Policy.* Hamden, Conn.: Archon Books, 1966. First published 1938.

———. *French Public Opinion and Foreign Affairs 1870–1914.* Hamden, Conn.: Archon Books, 1964. First published 1931.

Chevènement, Jean-Pierre. *France-Allemagne: parlons franc.* Paris: Plon, 1996.

Chickering, Roger. *We Men Who Feel Most German: A Cultural Study of the Pan-German League, 1886–1914.* Boston: George Allen and Unwin, 1984.

———. *Imperial Germany and a World without War: The Peace Movement and German Society, 1892–1914.* Princeton: Princeton University Press, 1976.

Christadler, Marieluise. *Kriegserziehung im Jugendbuch: Literarische Mobilmachung in Deutschland und Frankreich vor 1914.* Frankfurt am Main: Haag und Herchen, 1979.

Christadler, Marieliuse, ed. *Die geteilte Utopie: Sozialisten in Frankreich und Deutschland.* Opladen: Leske and Budrich, 1985.

———. *Deutschland, Frankreich: alte Klischees, neue Bilder.* Duisburg: Verlag der Sozialwissenschaftlichen Kooperative, 1981.

Clapham, J. H. *The Economic Development of France and Germany 1815–1914.* 4th ed. Cambridge: Cambridge University Press, 1951.

Clark, Linda L. *Social Darwinism in France.* University, Ala.: University of Alabama Press, 1984.

Cobb, Richard. *French and Germans, Germans and French: A Personal Interpretation of France under Two Occupations.* Hanover: University Press of New England, 1983.

Coetzee, Marilyn. *The German Army League: Popular Nationalism in Wilhelmine Germany.* Oxford: Oxford University Press, 1990.

Contamine, Henry. *La revanche 1871–1914.* Paris: Editions Berger-Levrault, 1957.

Crook, D. P. *Darwinism, War, and History: The Debate over the Biology of War from the 'Origin of Species' to the First World War.* Cambridge: Cambridge University Press, 1994.

Curtis, Michael. *Three Against the Third Republic: Sorel, Barrès, and Maurras.* Princeton: Princeton University Press, 1959.

Czempiel, Ernst Otto. *Das deutsche Dreyfus-Geheimnis: Eine Studie über den Einfluß des monarchischen Regierungssystems auf die Frankreichpolitik des Wilhelminischen Reiches.* Munich: Scherz Verlag, 1966.

De Mendelssohn, Peter. *Zeitungsstadt Berlin: Menschen und Mächte in der Geschichte der deutschen Presse.* Frankfurt a. M.: Ullstein, 1982.

Deutschland—Frankreich: Ein neues Kapitel ihrer Geschichte, 1948–1963–1993. Bonn: Europa Union Verlag, 1993.

Digeon, Claude. *La crise allemande de la pensée française 1870–1914.* Paris: Presses universitaires de France, 1959.

Distelbarth, Paul. *Das andere Frankreich.* Bern: P. Lang, 1997.

———. *Franzosen und Deutsche: Bauern und Krieger.* Stuttgart: Rowohlt Verlag, 1946.

Dörzbacher, Erwin. *Die deutsche Sozialdemokratie und die nationale Machtpolitik bis 1914.* Gotha: Perthes, 1920.

Drachkovitch, M. M. *Les socialismes français et allemand et le problème de la guerre 1870–1914.* Geneva: E. Droz, 1953.

Droz, Jacques. *Le socialisme allemand de 1869 à 1918.* Paris: Centre de Documentation Universitaire, 1970.

———. *Les relations franco-allemandes intellectuelles de 1871 à 1914.* Paris: Centre de Documentation Universitaire, 1966.

———. *Le nationalisme allemand de 1871 à 1939.* Paris: Centre de Documentation Universitaire, 1963.

Dülffer, Jost, and Karl Holl, eds. *Bereit zum Krieg: Kriegsmentalität im wilhelminischen Deutschland, 1890–1914.* Göttingen: Vandenhoeck and Ruprecht, 1986.

Dupuy, Aimé. *Sedan et l'enseignement de la revanche.* Paris: Institut national de recherche et de documentation pédagogiques, 1975.

Farrar, L. L. *The Short War Illusion: German Policy, Strategy and Domestic Affairs August–December 1914.* Santa Barbara: Clio Press, 1973.

Finkielkraut, Alain. *La défaite de la pensée.* Paris: Gallimard, 1987.

Firchow, Peter Edgerly. *The Death of the German Cousin: Variations on a Literary Stereotype, 1890–1920.* Lewisburg: Bucknell University Press, 1986.

Fischer, Fritz. *War of Illusions: German Policies from 1911 to 1914.* New York: W. W. Norton and Co., 1975.

———. *Germany's Aims in the First World War.* London: Norton, 1967.

———. "Das Bild Frankreichs in Deutschland in den Jahren vor dem Ersten Weltkrieg." *Revue d'Allemagne* 4, no. 3 (1972): 505ff. Reprinted in *Weltmacht oder Niedergang?* Frankfurt a. M.: Europäische Verlagsanstalt, 1965.

Flohr, Anne Katrin. *Feindbilder in der internationalen Politik: Ihre Entstehung und ihre Funktion.* Bonn: Lit Verlag, 1991.

François, Etienne, et al. *Nation und Emotion: Deutschland und Frankreich im Vergleich 19. und 20. Jahrhundert*. Göttingen: Vandenhoeck and Ruprecht, 1995.

François-Poncet, André. *De Versailles à Potsdam: la France et le problème allemand contemporain*. Paris: E. Flammarion, 1948.

Gall, Lothar. *Germania: Eine deutsche Marianne?* Bonn: Bouvier Verlag, 1993.

Gautier, Philippe. *La germanophobie*. Paris: L'Ancre, 1997.

Geiss, Imanuel. *Der lange Weg in die Katastrophe: Die Vorgeschichte des Ersten Weltkriegs 1815–1914*. Munich: Piper, 1990.

———. *German Foreign Policy, 1871–1914*. London: Routledge and Kegan Paul, 1976.

Geiss, Imanuel, and Bernd Jürgen Wendt, eds. *Deutschland in der Weltpolitik des 19. und 20. Jahrhunderts*. Düsseldorf: Bertelsmann Universitätsverlag, 1974.

Gervereau, Laurent, and Christophe Prochasson, eds. *L'Affaire Dreyfus et le tournant du siècle (1894–1910)*. Paris: Editions la Découverte, 1994.

Giesen, Bernhard. *Die Intellektuellen und die Nation: Eine deutsche Achsenzeit*. Frankfurt a. M.: Suhrkamp, 1993.

———. *Nationale und kulturelle Identität: Studien zur Entwicklung des kollektiven Bewußtseins in der Neuzeit*. Frankfurt a. M.: Suhrkamp, 1991.

Girardet, Raoul, ed. *Le nationalisme français, 1871–1914*. Paris: Editions du Seuil, 1983.

Glaudes, Pierre and Michel Malicet, eds. "Léon Bloy et la guerre de 1870 (autour de *Sueur de sang*)." *La Revue des lettres modernes* (1989).

Gödde-Baumanns, Beate. "Ansichten eines Krieges. Die 'Kriegsschuldfrage' von 1870 in zeitgenössischem Bewußtsein, Publizistik und wissenschaftlicher Diskussion 1870–1914." In Eberhard Kolb, ed., *Europa vor dem Krieg von 1870: Mächtekonstellation, Konfliktfelder, Kriegsausbruch*. Munich: R. Oldenbourg, 1987.

———. "L'idée des deux Allemagnes dans l'historiographie française des années 1871–1914." *Francia* 12 (1984): 609–619.

———. *Deutsche Geschichte in französischer Sicht: Die französische Historiographie von 1871 bis 1918 über die Geschichte Deutschlands und die deutsch-französischen Beziehungen in der Neuzeit*. Wiesbaden: Franz Steiner Verlag, 1971.

Goldberg, Harvey. *The Life of Jean Jaurès*. Madison: University of Wisconsin Press, 1962.

Gooch, G. P. *Franco-German Relations 1871–1914*. New York: Russell and Russell, 1922.

Groh, Dieter. *Negative Integration und revolutionärer Attentismus: Die deutsche Sozialdemokratie am Vorabend des Ersten Weltkrieges*. Frankfurt a. M.: Ullstein, 1973.

Grupp, Peter. *Deutschland, Frankreich und die Kolonien: Der französische "parti colonial" und Deutschland*. Tübingen: Mohr, 1980.

Guillen, Pierre. "Les questions coloniales dans les relations franco-allemandes à la veille de la première guerre mondiale." *Revue Historique* 268 (July–September 1972): 87–106.

Hale, Oron J. *Germany and the Diplomatic Revolution: A Study in Diplomacy and the Press, 1904–1906*. New York: Octagon Books, 1971; first published 1931.

Hall, Alex. *Scandal, Sensation and Social Democracy: The SPD Press and Wilhelmine Germany 1890–1914*. Cambridge: Cambridge University Press, 1977.

Hanschmidt, Alwin. "Die französisch-deutschen Parlamentarier-konferenzen von Bern (1913) und Basel (1914)." *Geschichte in Wissenschaft und Unterricht* 26, no. 6 (1975): 335–359.

Harcourt, Robert d'. *Les allemands d'aujourd'hui*. Paris: Librairie Hachette, 1948.

Haupt, Georges. *Socialism and the Great War: The Collapse of the Second International*. Oxford: Clarendon Press, 1972.

Hawkins, Mike. *Social Darwinism in European and American Thought 1860–1945*. Cambridge: Cambridge University Press, 1997.

Heidorn, Gunter. *Monopole, Presse, Krieg: Die Rolle der Presse bei der Vorbereitung des Ersten Weltkrieges*. Berlin [East]: Rutten and Loening, 1960.

Herrmann, David G. *The Arming of Europe and the Making of the First World War*. Princeton: Princeton University Press, 1996.

Herwig, Holger H. *The First World War: Germany and Austria-Hungary 1914–1918*. London: Arnold, 1997.

Hillgruber, Andreas. *Germany and the Two World Wars*. Trans. William C. Kirby. Cambridge: Harvard University Press, 1981.

Howard, Michael. *The Franco-Prussian War*. New York: Methuen, 1961.

Hull, Isabel. *The Entourage of Kaiser Wilhelm II, 1888–1918*. Cambridge: Cambridge University Press, 1982.

Jäckel, Eberhard. *Frankreich in Hitlers Europa: Die deutsche Frankreichpolitik im 2. Weltkrieg*. Stuttgart: Deutsche Verlags-Anstalt, 1966.

Janowitz, Morris, ed. *W. I. Thomas on Social Organization and Social Personality: Selected Papers*. Chicago: University of Chicago Press, 1966.

Jaspers, Karl. *Man in the Modern World*. Trans. by Eden and Cedar Paul. New York: Henry Holt and Co., 1933.

Jeismann, Michael. *Das Vaterland der Feinde: Studien zum nationalen Feindbegriff und Selbstverständnis in Deutschland und Frankreich 1792–1918*. Stuttgart: Klett-Cotta, 1992.

Joll, James. *The Second International 1889–1914*. New York: Harper and Row, 1966.

Kaelble, Hartmut. *Nachbarn am Rhein: Entfremdung und Annäherung der französischen und deutschen Gesellschaft seit 1880*. Munich: Beck, 1991.

———. "Die vergessene Gesellschaft im Westen? Das Bild der Deutschen von der französischen Gesellschaft, 1871–1914." *Revue d'Allemagne* 21, no. 2 (1989): 181–196.

Kaider, Gerhard R. "Der Bildungsbürger und die normative Kraft des Faktischen. 1870/71 im Urteil der deutschen Intelligenz." In Hans-Jürgen Lüsebrink and Janos Riesz, eds. *Feindbild und Faszination: Vermittlerfiguren und Wahrnehmungsprozesse in den deutsch-französischen Kulturbeziehungen 1789–1983*. Frankfurt a. M.: M. Diesterweg, 1984.

Keen, Sam. *Faces of the Enemy: Reflections of the Hostile Imagination*. San Francisco: Harper and Row, 1986.

Keiger, John F.V. *Raymond Poincaré*. Cambridge: Cambridge University Press, 1997.

———. *France and the Origins of the First World War*. New York: St. Martin's Press, 1983.

Kelly, Alfred. *The Descent of Darwin: The Popularization of Darwinism in Germany, 1860–1914*. Chapel Hill: University of North Carolina Press, 1981.

Kempf, Marcelle. *Romain Rolland et l'Allemagne*. Paris: Nouvelles Editions Debresse, 1962.

Keyserling, Hermann Alexander, Graf. *Das Spektrum Europas*. Heidelberg: Niels Kampmann Verlag, 1928.

Kitchen, Martin. *The German Officer Corps 1890–1914*. Oxford: Clarendon Press, 1968.

Knipping, Franz, and Ernst Weisenfeld, eds. *Eine ungewöhnliche Geschichte: Deutschland, Frankreich seit 1870*. Bonn: Europa Union Verlag, 1988.

H. W. Koch. *Der Sozialdarwinismus: Seine Genese und sein Einfluss auf das imperialistische Denken*. Munich: Beck, 1973.

Koch, H. W., ed. *The Origins of the First World War: Great Power Rivalry and German War Aims*. New York: Taplinger Publishing Co., 1972.

Kocka, Jürgen, and Mitchell, Allan, eds. *Bourgeois Society in Nineteenth-Century Europe*. Oxford, Providence: Berg, 1993.

Kohut, Thomas. *Wilhelm II and the Germans: A Study in Leadership*. Oxford: Oxford University Press, 1991.

———. "Mirror Image of the Nation: An Investigation of Kaiser Wilhelm II's Leadership of the Germans." In Charles B. Strozier and Daniel Offer, eds., *The Leader: Psychohistorical Essays*. New York: Plenum Press, 1985.

Krauss, Werner. "Deutschland als Thema der französischen Literatur." *Deutsche Vierteljahrschrift für Literaturwissenschaft und Geistesgeschichte* 11, no. 3 (1933): 445ff.

Kruck, Alfred. *Geschichte des Alldeutschen Verbandes, 1890–1939*. Wiesbaden: F. Steiner, 1954.

Krumeich, Gerd. "Le déclin de la France dans la pensée politique et militaire allemande avant la première guerre mondiale." In Jean-Claude Allain, ed., *La moyenne puissance au XXème siècle: recherche d'une définition*. Paris: FEDN-IHCC, 1989.

Lair, Maurice. *Jaurès et l'Allemagne*. Paris: Librairie Académique Perrin, 1935.

Langemeyer, Gerhard, ed. *Bilderwelten II: Satirische Illustrationen im Frankreich der Jahrhundertwende*. Dortmund: Cramers Kunstanstalt Verlag, 1986.

Langsam, Walter Consuelo. "Nationalism and History in the Prussian Elementary Schools under William II." In Edward Meade Earle, ed., *Nationalism and Internationalism*. New York: Columbia University Press, 1950.

Lauret, René. *France and Germany: The Legacy of Charlemagne*. Chicago: H. Regnery, 1964.

Leiner, Wolfgang. *Das Deutschlandbild in der französischen Literatur*. Darmstadt: Wissenschaftliche Buchgesellschaft, 1989.

Lethève, Jacques. *La caricature et la presse sous la IIIe République*. Paris: A. Colin, 1961.

Levillain, Philippe, and Rainer Riemenschneider, eds. *La guerre de 1870/71 et ses conséquences: actes du XXe Colloque historique franco-allemand*. Bonn: Bouvier, 1990.

L'Huillier, Fernand. *Dialogues franco-allemandes 1925–1933*. Strasbourg: Publications de la faculté des lettres de l'université de Strasbourg, 1971.

Lichtenberger, Henri. *Relations between France and Germany* (Washington: The Carnegie Endowment, 1923).

Linsel, Knut. *Charles de Gaulle und Deutschland*. Sigmaringen: J. Thorbecke, 1998.

Lipiansky, Edmond Marc. "L'imagerie de l'identité: le couple France-Allemagne." *Ethnopsychologie* 34, no. 3/4 (1979): 273–282.

Maxelon, Michael-Olaf. *Stresemann und Frankreich 1914–1929: Deutsche Politik der Ost-West-Balance*. Düsseldorf: Droste Verlag, 1972.

May, Ernest R., ed. *Knowing One's Enemies: Intelligence Assessment before the Two World Wars*. Princeton: Princeton University Press, 1984.

Mayeur, Jean Marie. *Autonomie et politique en Alsace: la constitution de 1911*. Paris: A. Colin, 1970.

Meyer, Thomas. *"Endlich eine Tat, eine befreiende Tat"*: *Alfred von Kiderlen-Wächters "Panthersprung nach Agadir" unter dem Druck der öffentlichen Meinung.* Husum: Matthiesen Verlag, 1996.

Michalka, Wolfgang, ed. *Der Erste Weltkrieg: Wirkung, Wahrnehmung, Analyse.* Munich: Piper Verlag, 1994.

Michel, Henri, et al. *La France et l'Allemagne 1932–1936.* Paris: Editions du Centre National de la Recherche Scientifique, 1980.

Miller, Michael B. *Shanghai on the Metro: Spies, Intrigue, and the French between the Wars.* Berkeley: University of California Press, 1994.

Milza, Pierre, and Raymond Poidevin, eds. *La puissance française à la "Belle Epoque": mythe ou réalité?* Paris: Editions Complexe, 1992.

Mitchell, Allan. *The Divided Path: The German Influence on Social Reform in France after 1870.* Chapel Hill: University of North Carolina Press, 1991.

———. *Victors and Vanquished: The German Influence on Army and Church in France after 1870.* Chapel Hill: University of North Carolina Press, 1984.

———. "The Xenophobic Style: French Counterespionage and the Emergence of the Dreyfus Affair." *Journal of Modern History* 52 (September 1980): 414–425.

———. "German History in France after 1870." *Journal of Contemporary History* 2, no. 3 (1967): 81–100.

Mitterrand, François. *De l'Allemagne, de la France.* Paris: Editions O. Jacob, 1996.

Mommsen, W. J. "Kurt Riezler, ein Intellektueller im Dienste Wilhelminischer Machtpolitik." *Geschichte in Wissenschaft und Unterricht* 25, no. 4 (1974): 193–209.

Monnet, François. *Refaire la république: André Tardieu, une dérive réactionaire (1876–1945).* Paris: A. Fayard, 1993.

Nietzsche, Friedrich. "David Strauss, the Confessor and the Writer," *Untimely Meditations.* Trans. and ed. by R. J. Hollingdale; Cambridge: Cambridge University Press, 1983).

Nora, Pierre. "Ernest Lavisse: son rôle dans la formation du sentiment national." *Revue historique* 228 (July–September 1962): 73–106.

Nora, Pierre, ed. *Les lieux de mémoire.* Paris: Gallimard, 1984–.

Nurdin, Jean. "Images de la France en Allemagne 1870–1970." *Ethno-psychologie* 26, no. 4 (1971): 389–414.

Ohler, Norbert. *Deutschland und die deutsche Frage in der "Revue des Deux Mondes" 1905–1940: Ein Beitrag zur Erhellung des französischen Deutschlandbildes.* Frankurt a. M.: Akademische Verlagsgesellschaft, 1973.

Oncken, Emily. *Panthersprung nach Agadir: Die deutsche Politik während der zweiten Marokkokrise 1911.* Düsseldorf: Droste Verlag, 1981.

Ozouf, Mona. *L'école de la France: essais sur la Révolution, l'utopie et l'enseignement.* Paris: Editions Gallimard, 1984.

Poidevin, Raymond. "Wirtschaftlicher und finanzieller Nationalismus in Frankreich und Deutschland 1907–1914." *Geschichte in Wissenschaft und Unterricht* (March 1974): 150–162.

———. "La question d'un rapprochement économique et financier entre la France et l'Allemagne de 1906 à 1909." *Revue d'Allemagne* 4, no. 3 (1972).

———. *Les relations économiques et financières entre la France et l'Allemagne de 1898 à 1914.* Paris: Comité pour l'histoire économique et financière de la France, 1969.

Poidevin, Raymond, and Jacques Bariéty. *Les Relations franco-allemands 1815–1975.* Paris: Armand Colin, 1977.

Posse, Paul. *Die Boches: Eine Culturschande in System gebracht (Eindrucksvoll vertieft durch Meisterwerke der künstlerischen Sektion für Bochologie).* Gedruckt im Narrenmond. Leipzig: Georg Kummers Verlag, 1928.

Raithel, Thomas. *Das "Wunder" der inneren Einheit: Studien zur deutschen und französischen Öffentlichkeit bei Beginn des Ersten Weltkrieges.* Bonn: Bouvier Verlag, 1996.

Raulff, Heiner. *Zwischen Machtpolitik und Imperialismus: Die deutsche Frankreichpolitik 1904–1906.* Düsseldorf: Droste Verlag, 1976.

Renouvin, Pierre. "Les relations franco-allemandes de 1871 à 1914: Esquisse d'un programme de recherches." In A. O. Sarkissian, ed., *Studies in Diplomatic History and Historiography in Honor of G. P. Gooch.* New York: Barnes and Noble, 1962.

Reshef, Ouriel. *Guerre, mythes et caricature: au berceau d'une mentalité française.* Paris: Presses de la Fondation Nationale des Sciences Politiques, 1984.

Richtering, Gerhard, ed. *Deutschland—Frankreich: Höhen und Tiefen einer Zweierbeziehung.* Essen: Verlag Die Blaue Eule, 1988.

Rieber, Robert W., ed. *The Psychology of War and Peace: The Image of the Enemy.* New York: Plenum Press, 1991.

Rieger, Isolde. *Die Wilhelminische Presse im Überblick 1888–1918.* Munich: Pohl, 1957.

Rohkramer, Thomas. "Der Gesinnungsmilitarismus der 'kleinen Leute' im Deutschen Kaiserreich." In Wolfram Wette, ed., *Der Krieg des kleinen Mannes: Eine Militärgeschichte von Unten.* Munich: Piper, 1992.

———. *Der Militarismus der "kleinen Leute": die Kriegervereine im Deutschen Kaiserreich 1871–1914.* Munich: R. Oldenbourg, 1990.

Ropponen, Risto. *Die russische Gefahr: Das Verhalten der öffentlichen Meinung Deutschlands und Österreich-Ungarns gegenüber der Aussenpolitik Russlands in der Zeit zwischen dem Frieden von Portsmouth und dem Ausbruch des Ersten Weltkriegs.* Helsinki: Forssa, 1976.

Ruhn, Joachim, ed. *Der Nationalismus im Leben der Dritten Republik.* Berlin: Baetel, 1920.

Sagave, Pierre-Paul. *1871 Berlin-Paris.* Frankfurt a. M.: Ullstein, 1971.

Schallenberger, Horst. *Untersuchungen zum Geschichtsbild der Wilhelminischen Ära und der Weimarer Zeit.* Ratingen bei Düsseldorf: A. Henn, 1964.

Schilling, Konrad. *Beiträge zu einer Geschichte des radikalen Nationalismus in der Wilhelminischen Ära.* Cologne: Gouder and Hansen, 1968.

Schmidt, Madeleine, ed. *Chansons de la revanche et de la grande guerre.* Nancy: Presses universitaires de Nancy, 1985.

Schockenhoff, Andreas. *Henri Albert und das Deutschlandbild des Mercure de France, 1890–1905.* Frankfurt a. M.: P. Lang, 1986.

Schoenbaum, David. *Zabern 1913: Consensus Politics in Imperial Germany.* London: George Allen and Unwin, 1982.

Schorske, Carl E. *German Social Democracy 1905–1917: The Development of the Great Schism.* Cambridge: Harvard University Press, 1955.

Schuker, Stephen. *The End of French Predominance in Europe: The Financial Crisis of 1924 and the Adoption of the Dawes Plan.* Chapel Hill: The University of North Carolina Press, 1976.

Schwarz, Hans-Peter. *Erbfreundschaft: Adenauer und Frankreich.* Bonn: Bouvier, 1992.

Seager, Frederic H. "The Alsace-Lorraine Question in France, 1871–1914." In Charles K. Warner, ed., *From the Ancien Regime to the Popular Front*. New York: Columbia University Press, 1969.

Shamir, Haim, ed. *France and Germany in an Age of Crisis 1900–1960*. Leiden: E. J. Brill, 1990.

Sieloff, Charles Gustav. "France and Weltpolitik: The Image and Role of France in German Public Opinion, 1911–14." Ph.D. diss., Stanford University, 1970.

Siepe, Hans T. "Die Höhle des Drachen und das Herz der Hölle: Zur Mythologisierung des Ruhrgebiets in der französischen Literatur zwischen 1870 und 1923." In Michel Grunewald and Jochen Schlobach, eds., *Médiations: aspects des relations franco-allemandes du XVIIe siècle à nos jours*. Vol. 1. Bern, New York: P. Lang, 1992.

Silverman, Dan P. *Reluctant Union: Alsace-Lorraine and Imperial Germany 1871–1918*. University Park: Pennsylvania State University Press, 1972.

Stargardt, Nicholas. *The German Idea of Militarism: Radical and Socialist Critics, 1866–1914*. Cambridge: Cambridge University Press, 1994.

Sternhell, Zeev. *La droite révolutionnaire: les origines françaises du fascisme 1885–1914*. Paris: Editions du Seuil, 1978.

———. *Maurice Barrès et le nationalisme français*. Paris: A. Colin, 1972.

Stevenson, David. *Armaments and the Coming of War: Europe, 1904–1914*. Oxford: Clarendon Press, 1996.

Teitelbaum, Michael S., and Jay M. Winter. *The Fear of Population Decline*. Orlando: Academic Press, 1985.

Teven, Leonhard. *Der Deutsche im französischen Roman seit 1870*. Weilburg-Lahn: Zipper, 1915.

Thompson, Wayne C. *In the Eye of the Storm: Kurt Riezler and the Crises of Modern Germany*. Iowa City: University of Iowa Press, 1980.

Tiemann, Dieter. *Frankreich- und Deutschlandbilder im Widerstreit: Urteile französischer und deutscher Schüler über die Nachbarn am Rhein*. Bonn: Europa Union, 1982.

Ullrich, Gunter. *Das Ende einer Rivalität? Perspektiven zur deutsch-französischen Verständigung*. Lindhorst: Askania, 1986.

Uthmann, Jorg von. *Le diable est-il allemand?: 200 ans de préjugés franco-allemands*. Paris: Denoel, 1984.

Vandenrath, Johannes, et al. *1914: Les psychoses de guerre*. Mont-Saint-Aignan: Publications de l'Université de Rouen, 1985.

Weber, Eugen. *Peasants into Frenchmen: The Modernization of Rural France, 1870–1914*. Stanford: Stanford University Press, 1976.

———. *The Nationalist Revival in France, 1905–1914*. Berkeley: University of California Press, 1959.

Wehler, Hans-Ulrich. *Krisenherde des Kaiserreichs 1871–1918*. Göttingen: Vandenhoeck and Ruprecht, 1970.

Weigel, Hans, Walter Lukan, and Max D. Peyfuss. *Jeder Schuss ein Russ, jeder Stoss ein Franzos: Literarische und graphische Kriegspropaganda in Deutschland und Österreich 1914–1918*. Vienna: Edition Christian Brandstätter, 1983.

Wernecke, Klaus. *Der Wille zur Weltgeltung: Aussenpolitik und Öffentlichkeit im Kaiserreich am Vorabend des Ersten Weltkrieges*. Düsseldorf: Droste, 1970.

Wild, Adolf. *Baron d'Estournelles de Constant (1852–1924): Das Wirken eines Friedensnobelpreisträgers für die deutsch-französische Verständigung und europäische Einigung*. Hamburg: Fundament-Verlag Sasse, 1973.

Wilsberg, Klaus. *"Terrible ami—aimable ennemi": Kooperation und Konflikt in den deutsch-französischen Beziehungen 1911–1914.* Bonn: Bouvier Verlag, 1998.

Winock, Michel. *Nationalisme, antisémitisme et fascisme en France.* Paris: Editions du Seuil, 1990.

Wolfzettel, Friedrich. "Das entzauberte Deutschland: Französische Reiseberichte zwischen 1870 und 1914." In Hans T. Siepe, ed., *Grenzgänge: Kulturelle Begegnungen zwischen Deutschland und Frankreich.* Essen: Die Blaue Eule, 1988.

Young, Harry F. *Maximilian Harden, censor Germaniae: The Critic in Opposition from Bismarck to the Rise of Nazism.* The Hague: M. Nijhoff, 1959.

Ziebura, Gilbert. *Die deutsch-französischen Beziehungen seit 1945: Mythen und Realitäten.* Rev. ed. Stuttgart: Neske, 1997.

———. *Die deutsche Frage in der öffentlichen Meinung Frankreichs von 1911–1914.* Berlin-Dahlem: Colloquium Verlag, 1955.

Žižek, Slavoj. *Did Somebody Say Totalitarianism? Five Interventions in the (Mis)use of a Notion.* London and New York: Verso, 2001.

INDEX